Y0-BRV-076

3900 WINDSOR HALL DRIVE
WILLIAMSBURG, VIRGINIA 23188

CALL ME B

A HOPEFUL VIEW OF HISTORY AND THE REVOLUTION

BILL BRYANT

WILLIAMSBURG
VIRGINIA

On the cover: In this 2007 photograph by the Richmond
            Times-Dispatch, the ship Godspeed sails
            up the James River with Richmond in the
            distance.

Published by
The Educational Publisher Inc.
Biblio Publishing
Biblio Publishing.com

ISBN: 978-1-62249-235-0

CONTENTS

MAYANS ET AL
SCENES ALONG THE PIER

"WHAT DO YOU DO IN REAL LIFE?"
DIVERSITY
CUBBIES ET AL
VETERANS
RELIGION
"POLITICS" AND "REVOLUTION"

EVALUATIONS
FEEDBACK
INFLUENCE
FULL DISCLOSURE

Remember . . .

"As we would have our descendants judge us, so we ought to judge our fathers. In order to form a correct estimate of their merits, we ought to place ourselves in their situation, to put out of our minds, for a time, all that knowledge which they could not have and we could not help having . . . It is too much that the benefactors of mankind, after having been reviled by the dunces of their generation for going too far, should be reviled by the dunces of the next generation for not going far enough."

Thomas B. Macauley

THANKS AND DISCLAIMERS

SOME THANKS

- To my wife Dot and son Michael for assisting me invaluably in the preparation of this manuscript (meaning I don't know anywhere near enough about computers), with extra thanks to Michael for research help.

- To several of my colleagues, especially Suzanne DuBois, for reviewing this manuscript to determine approximately how many errors I have made; and to several other friends, especially Paul Aron and my cousin Ken Dobyns, for making helpful suggestions.

- To the following for assisting me with particular research questions: Ed Ayers, Lynn DiVito, Keith Egloff, Nancy Egloff, Dan Hawks, Ray Hoyle, Don Hulick and Tracy Perkins of the Jamestown-Yorktown Foundation, Juleigh Clark at the Colonial Williamsburg Foundation, Jennie Davy at the Swem Library of the College of William and Mary, Kristi Finefield at the Library of Congress, Robin Snelson at the Space Studies Institute, Richard Sorensen and Eric Grace at the Smithsonian Institution, bibliophile Tennyson

Williams and longtime friend and space visionary Charlie Chafer.

SOME DISCLAIMERS

- I have written this book not as an employee of the Jamestown-Yorktown Foundation, but as a private citizen who happens to work there part-time. Accordingly, the sentiments and opinions I express are my own and should not be viewed as reflecting the policy of the Jamestown-Yorktown Foundation or any of its employees, volunteers or donors, although I naturally entertain the hope that most if not all of my colleagues share many if not all of my sentiments and opinions, or at least respect them.

- I disclaim being perfect, and accept responsibility for any errors of fact or limitations of understanding found in this book, and would appreciate being corrected.

- This is not a kiss-and-tell book. It is, however, a hug-and-tell book. Be prepared.

- This is not exactly a book about history, or about teaching and learning methodologies, or educational theory and practice, or museum operations, or politics or revolution or the future.

It's about all of these things, and more, because it's a book about people.

- I am not as vain and egotistical as some parts of this book might make you believe I must be. In deciding what to put in and what to leave out, I have been guided by the compelling purpose of the book – to teach, from lessons I have learned through personal experience as well as academic study – even if, to make a point effectively, I must shed modesty. Some of my friends, through the years, have criticized me for not being more ego-asserting and self-promotional. This book will please them, even as it makes me uncomfortable.

A Thought for Today

The American war is over, but this is
far from the case with the American Revolution.
On the contrary, nothing but the first act
of the great drama is closed.

Benjamin Rush
Signer of the Declaration of Independence

The struggle of today is not altogether for today.
It is for a vast future, also.
Abraham Lincoln

CHAPTER 1: PRELUDE

AN INCIDENT

To explain why at the age of 72 I felt compelled to begin writing this book, I must refer to the manner of my early education in history, and to a specific moment in my youth.

I became addicted to the study of history – past and present and future – soon after I learned to read. In this, I was aided and abetted by my history-loving uncle Gordon Mason, who introduced me to the wonders of musty antique stores and their dusty old books – Gibbon, Mommsen, Keightley, Rollins and scores of other mostly 19th century tellers of the human story, with their richness of detail and distinctive interpretations and complex writing styles. Biographies and plans of battle and courses of empire fascinated me. My earliest "hero" was Hannibal, whom I admire not just for his military genius, but even more for his leadership, fully sharing the hardships and dangers of his men.

1

With similar enthusiasm, I read books about more recent history and learned early to scan the daily newspapers and the weekly news magazines. I started becoming acquainted with World War II soon after it happened, and I acutely studied the Korean War, which raged while my father was stationed with the Navy at Norfolk and then on Long Island.

If in this zeal for history I was unconventional, and a bit more serious-minded than other children, I certainly shared with them one characteristic: I wondered about the future.

In April of 1953, I was 12, beginning the walk home from Freeport Junior High, when I was impacted by two thoughts almost simultaneously – Thought 1: *Humanity is heading toward a great systemic crisis someday.* Thought 2: *If I prepare myself, I could be of service when that day comes.*

It happened in a couple of seconds. And from that day to this, the course of my life has been governed by the dictates of that moment.

* * *

This is not an autobiography. Suffice it to say that during the years since then I have been preoccupied with learning more about the distant and recent past, observing current events, studying new subjects, trying to keep track of advances in science and technology, obtaining and sharing useful skills and knowledge, helping to organize people to deal with community tasks, trying to be of public service – always with an eye to the future. Sometimes, this preoccupation has caused me to neglect family and friends, which I deeply regret.

Throughout the intervening years, the purpose of my life has remained constant while the path of my life has been diverted and redirected many times by a wide variety of circumstances, two early examples of which suggest how easily a different path might have distracted me from the purpose:

- As a freshman at Woodrow Wilson High in Portsmouth, Virginia, I eagerly anticipated being in an actual ancient history class. Within a week, it became apparent that I knew more about the subject than the teacher, who for the rest of the year allowed me to sit in the back of the room reading the morning newspaper, interrupting me only when there was a question she could not answer. She and the principal wrote a letter to the producers of "The $64,000 Question" recommending me as a contestant. Thank God, there was no reply . . . Thus undistracted as a sophomore, being very shy but knowing that to prepare myself I must learn how to speak well, I joined the debate team. As a junior, knowing I must learn how to write well, I joined the newspaper staff.

- As a senior at Wilson, I told the track coach I wanted to quit the debate team and run the mile. He, being the last state debate champion in the school's history, refused to let me join the track team, declaring: "Your job in life is to **think**, not run." That spring, instead of running a mediocre mile, I (also the school newspaper editor) together with my partner Deliaan Angel (also the school yearbook editor) won the state affirmative debate championship. Thanks, Coach, and Deliaan.

Into the 1960s and during the 1970s, the 1980s and the 1990s, I stayed on the sometimes bewildering path set in the springtime of '53 . . . always wondering about the future, studying it.

* * *

In February of 1999, I was sitting in my chair, reading the newspaper, minding my own business, when my wife Dot stuck in front of my face a freshly clipped classified ad and announced simply: "We need more money."

One glance at the ad – something about a "museum program assistant" at Jamestown Settlement – made me unhappy, but I said nothing and merely nodded, because she was right.

I objected to the idea because it would (1) distract me from my focus on my book about Nat

Turner, (2) require me to enter a whole new working environment peopled by strangers, and (3) engage me in activity not directly related to public service at (4) a place about which I knew little and much of the little I knew, admittedly from its earlier years, was unfavorable. All of which was heavily outweighed by (5): "We need more money."

I could not have been more wrong in my objections and expectations. Today, on my résumé, my time with the Jamestown-Yorktown Foundation is regarded as "Public Service" – and I happen to consider it one of my best contributions to the future, as well as a blessing to myself.

Among my reasons for feeling so fortunate:

- Not only did my book about Nat Turner proceed to publication as **Tomorrow Jerusalem**, but also my book of poetry **the 30th of may: a poem of the revolution** was published thanks to Phil Merrick, whom I met and befriended at Jamestown Settlement.

- The whole new working environment proved to be exciting, peopled by strangers who soon became like family, linked by a common love. Contact with people – colleagues and visitors alike – has been a kaleidoscopically changing yet continually pleasant experience.

- I have indeed been directly engaged in important public service.

- I have enjoyed it!!!

- I now know intimately Jamestown Settlement and the Yorktown Victory Center, and am proud to be serving at such first-class teaching institutions.

- I now know and understand fairly well the whole story and meaning of early Jamestown and the whole story and meaning of Yorktown, which I honestly did not know or understand anywhere near well enough in 1999, when I had to begin teaching and explaining the stories to other people.

- Having been a longtime close but outside observer of the tourism business in the Historic Triangle, suddenly I was in the belly of the beast, where for almost 15 years I have been learning not only about museum operations and the inner dynamics of the tourism business, but also about the sorts of people who visit this region, and why. (One thing I've learned to my dismay, as to the dismay of others, is that too many visitors, especially young people, have been leaving this area talking more about their "ghost tour" experiences in the restored area than about the living human **meaning** of our historic sites.)

- Being a revolutionist requires one to try to be very close to the whole people, a form of "research" which with my limited resources was for many years very difficult. This changed dramatically in 1999, when, instead of me searching for ways to learn how folks are really feeling out there in America and the world, the folks – the democracy – began coming to me! By the tens of thousands, from virtually every walk of life, from every state in the Union and scores of other nations, people from all along the spectrum of political and religious and economic and social experience have crossed my path since 1999, and many of them have shared their thoughts and feelings with me. I may be forgiven my honest belief that I understand the mood of the American people perhaps as well as anyone.

- I am smarter. I am wiser. I am a better person.

- I have helped to pay some bills.

- I have been enabled to write this book, which is supposedly about my experiences as a museum tour guide, but is really about what more than six decades of studying history with a purpose have taught me.

A CERTAIN BIAS

Whenever we express an opinion, we indicate a bias of some sort. Since the word "certain" means not only particular but also definite, and since I have a lot of opinions, I must acknowledge a certain fundamental bias in my point of view; numerous fundamental biases, actually, among them:

- Trained and experienced as an old-school journalist and competitive debater, I am biased toward objectivity, reasoning, analysis and fairness in my decision-making and judgment. (In debate, I much preferred the affirmative side – defining the terms, stating the compelling need for a major change in the current system to solve a major problem, and offering a workable plan to get the job done.)

- I am biased constantly toward the moderate center, preferably toward discussion rather than debate, always toward civility rather than hostility, cooperation rather than confrontation.

- I profess the bias of being an idealist **and** a realist, and am at ease being both. As long as my feet are on the ground, I am free to reach and dream as high as I want and wish and can, and free to encourage others to do so.

- I am biased toward the ideals of the American Revolution, the egalitarian sentiments of the Declaration of Independence and the promises of the Constitution and the Bill of Rights.

- I am a native son of Virginia, invested with the legacy of many generations of hard-working people, mostly of the yeoman class. In my manner, in my regard for history and in my attitude toward public service, I have always considered myself a Virginian. It is a state of mind, a sense of self and place and duty I have felt for as long as I can remember, re-enforced as I became familiar with the likes of Washington, Henry, Jefferson, Randolph, Wythe, Mason, Madison, Monroe, Marshall, Wilson and their ilk – and, I must add, influenced in more recent years by the spirit of the more native people of Virginia. (I feel I should note that my sense of being a Virginian was already well developed when as a young adult I began to learn about the ancestors I'll mention later in this book. And only very recently did I learn about my earliest Virginia ancestors; frankly, the new information stunned me – and I am not easily or often stunned.)

- I am certainly an optimist. History has taught me to be an optimist. I have no choice in the matter. I think things are going to turn out all right in the end. If there was ever any doubt in my mind, it was resolved in 1974 when (1) I perceived a fundamental promising shift in the course of human events, and (2) I attended a local lecture by a Princeton University physicist trying to arouse grassroots interest in a whole new way of looking at the future of human activity in space – a radical, logical alternative to the idea of merely bouncing clumsily around on the Moon

- I am most definitely biased toward the people, the whole people, to whom I feel a loyalty demanding absolute nonpartisanship and sometimes bordering on fanaticism. I make no apologies for this bias, or this devotion, although I probably should express regrets if I have disappointed some people or inadvertently stepped on some toes in the process of being so stubbornly nonpartisan.

CHALLENGING AXIOMS

Upon meeting Einstein, the great journalist Lincoln Steffens (whose autobiography is one of the best books I've ever read) asked: "How did you do it?"

Einstein answered: "By challenging an axiom."

I challenge four, beginning with:

Axiom 1
Humanity is heading toward some sort of cataclysmic disaster in the relatively near future.

Says who?

Hollywood! The popular media! The video game industry! Disaster sells, and if in the process of being profitable it darkens the mood and obscures the vision of the people, well, that's the price we pay for democracy and the free market, et cetera.

In fact, according to my research, humanity faces no immediate problems we cannot solve, if we cooperate, if common sense and common interest prevail. It all depends on the people, and I have faith in the people.

Likewise in fact, there are many less violent, more promising scenarios for the near-term and long-term future of humanity – great material, someday, for the game-makers, the film-makers, the image-makers. To make the future interesting and appealing, Klingons and killer asteroids are not required. Neither is:

Axiom 2
The need to make war
is inherent in human nature;
therefore, there will always be wars.

If this was ever true, and I doubt it, I am convinced it is no longer so. The improving conduct of nations, the inexorable surge of democracy, the greater maturity of humanity and the integrating effects of information technology and economics combine to put the abolition of war between nations, and of most others forms of war, within the reach of humanity well before the end of this century, and perhaps much sooner. We may dare to imagine it. It's what almost all of the people want.

The basic impulse of humanity is to create, not destroy. Peace is not a pause between wars; war is an interruption of peace. The fundamental path of the people through the ages has been forward and upward, not backward and downward. And when I think of the struggle of those people, to help us get to where we are today and might be tomorrow, it strengthens my resolve and as well as my confidence in the ability of the people.

Achieving peace will involve an end to:

Axiom 3
The resources of Earth are finite, increasing competition for diminishing resources, enhancing the prospect of war.

This mindset became global at the governmental level in the early 1970s due to publication of **The Limits of Growth**, and remains a widespread way of thinking even though its premises were shattered decades ago.

The resources of Earth are indeed finite. However, the resources available in space – including all of the raw materials found on Earth plus endless energy – are virtually infinite. And we already have, or soon can have, the technological ability to begin using these resources to the great advantage of the whole of humanity.

As that Princeton physicist and I wrote in 1980, for the First Global Conference on the Future: "We should be moving from an economics of scarcity to an economics of plenty, from competition for decreasing resources to cooperation for increasing resources. The challenge is to create a new capability for incorporating this dramatic new reality . . . In the final analysis, ours is the historic responsibility of unlocking the door to an open future for humanity."

The *real* breakout into space – like the proper response to most problems confronting humanity – is a global responsibility, a global task. The ability of the United States to assume a proper, necessary and appropriate role in this adventure will depend on how we deal with:

Axiom 4
The apathy of the American people contributes to the continuation of the crisis in governance.

The people are **not** apathetic. They care, a lot. But they feel helpless, uncomfortably divided, misled – respectful of our revolutionary ideals and constitutional form of government but unable to see **how** to change our obviously failing but entrenched system of electing those who administer the government.

There's a huge difference between apathy and helplessness. There is no cure for the former; for the latter, there is the continuing American Revolution, which I shall discuss later.

In the meantime, I refer to something Abraham Lincoln said in a different context but with a message directly relevant to today: "Revolutionize through the ballot-box, and restore the government once more to the affection and hearts of men, by making it express, as it was intended to do, the highest spirit of justice and liberty."

THE JOB

I am an MPA – a museum program assistant, a tour guide, a teacher – at Jamestown Settlement and the Yorktown Victory Center, administered by the Jamestown-Yorktown Foundation, an agency of the Department of Education of the Commonwealth of Virginia.

Thus, I am an employee of the people.

As of mid-December in 2014, I have taught 2,115 groups at Jamestown and 370 at Yorktown – very approximately 65,000 people.

Thus, I am a veteran, although it must be noted that in unwritten policy any MPA who survives one busy season is officially a veteran.

* * *

Before I came to work at Jamestown Settlement, I had never set foot inside the museum. The closest I got was the great lawn, where in 1984 (when the place was known as Jamestown Festival Park), as part of the 350th anniversary of James City County, I helped to produce a children's play I had been asked to write: "The Dreams of Today" a pleasant memory.

I don't remember much about the beginning of my formal (indoor and outdoor) training to be an MPA, except that the weather was unkindly cold and the training itself was considerably more

15

comprehensive, detailed and competent than I expected, though I must note that I really didn't know what to expect.

I emphasize: That was only the beginning of the training, which has been constant – at team meetings, general staff meetings, Training Academy courses ranging from terrorism awareness to archaeology, roundtable discussions, lecture series – plus the regular State of the Foundation briefings by executive director Phil Emerson (actually six presentations at times and places enabling almost all personnel to be updated and on the same page regarding a wide range of subjects). When I started training, I had no conception it would be like this.

Early on, personally and professionally, I felt comfortable among the people with whom I was working, particularly the veteran MPAs and the veteran costumed interpreters. It was obvious that they *wanted* to be there, *enjoyed* doing their jobs and *respected* one another, which, needless to say, makes for a good workplace. On a human level, the outlook was promising.

* * *

I remember only one thing about my first tour at the Settlement. I remember it distinctly because I have repeated it in one version or another on every tour I have given since, whatever the group's composition.

That first time, it happened to be an elementary school group.

"My name is Bill Bryant," I said, then impulsively added: "But if you have any questions for me today, please call me B. Let me hear it!"

"B!" the kids enthusiastically replied.

"Oh, that sounded good. Let me hear it again!!"

"B!!"

"Yes! One more time!!!"

"B!!!"

"Thank you . . . I have four grandchildren, who have always called me B. So if you call me B, who will I think of?"

"Your grandchildren."

"Will that make me happy?"

"Yes."

"And do you want a happy teacher?"

"Yes."

"Then what's my name?!"

"B!!!"

* * *

At a recent staff meeting, a new MPA commented that she kept asking herself: What am I doing here?

Amid mild laughter, I and other veterans exchanged glances and knowing nods. We are *still* asking ourselves that question!

I do hope this book helps to answer it.

The INTRODUCTION

!

First, you got to get their attention; then, you got to keep it. This is simpler with groups of adults, who know how to learn and to enjoy, than it is with groups of students, who are easily distracted and often need to be convinced that something is actually worth learning *and* can be enjoyed.

As soon as I begin to get together with a school group, while we're getting our first impressions of each other, I seek to establish bonds with them, for my sake as well as theirs.

Sometimes, my first words are stern instructions: "Okay, I have two rules. Here they come. Are you ready?" Some say yes; a few say yes, sir. "Don't call me sir. I'm a working man. I said are you ready?" Yes! "Are you ready?" Yes!!! "Rule number one: When I walk, you follow. If you get ahead of me, I will stop on a dime. You got that?" Yes! "Rule number two: When I stop to talk, you come close. I *have* stopped." They come closer. Sometimes, seeing a girl smiling, I sourly ask: "Why are you smiling? History isn't fun!" She and/or some classmates say yes, it is! "Okay," I immediately agree, smiling, changing my mind and my manner entirely. "In fact, history is the most fun subject there is. Do you know why? What's history all about? Us. And is there anything more exciting and interesting than us?" End of discussion.

Sometimes, we simply begin with the "B" routine.

* * *

At the beginning of (and throughout) all tours, I make emphatic the importance of the history we're talking about. Depending on the time available and the group's level of knowledge and understanding, this emphasis is expressed in various ways; but it is always there.

Consider:

- This is **not** Virginia history. This is **not** American history. This is **world** history, because what happened here – at Jamestown and at Williamsburg and at Yorktown – changed the whole world fundamentally, forever, and explains the world in which we live today.

- If we go back 400 years, to the time of early Jamestown, the *whole* world was ruled by a handful of powerful men mostly – kings, emperors, tsars, shahs, shoguns, whatever – and what did **we** count for? Let me hear you say: Zilch! Nada! Diddleysquat! And I'm being perfectly serious. The world was ruled by ignorance, poverty, oppression and a handful of powerful men, and we counted for nothing. That's the way it *was*, and it all began to change at Jamestown.

- In a roomful of a hundred English men 400 years ago, most of them could not read or write, and few of them could quality to vote in an election. In a roomful of a hundred English women, even fewer could read and write, and none could ever vote . . . Nowadays, 400 years of democracy later, how many of you know how to read and write? Get your hands up. How many of you know how to google? Keep 'em up. How many of you have at your fingertips in a second almost all of the knowledge of our species? "And **she,**" I say, pointing at a randomly chosen girl, "can be elected President of the United States!" That's the way it *is*. "Does that thought scare you?" I ask the chosen one. Whatever the reply, I say: "Scares *me*." And there is laughter, which is a good thing.

- When people go home from here, I want them to know exactly where they've been, unlike Columbus, who didn't have a clue. This is the Historic Triangle of Virginia – Jamestown, Williamsburg, Yorktown – three of modern history's most important sites, remarkably within a dozen miles of one another.

- Where did Virginia begin? Here's a hint: The answer begins with "J" and ends in "amestown" – Let me hear it. "Jamestown." Where Virginia began is especially important, considering Virginia's early reputation, prominence and influence.

- Where did the United States begin? "Jamestown."

- Where did the spread of the English language (not to mention English law and custom and culture) around the world begin? "Jamestown."

- Finally, the big question, the reason why millions of people come to this part of Virginia every year from every state in the nation and virtually every nation on the face of the Earth: Where in America was the seed of democracy planted? "Jamestown." Aha, but do you really know what "democracy" is? Think so? Then answer this: Who *rules* in the United States? Who's the *boss* of us? No, not the President, not Obama, not the government. *We* **are the boss of us.** And never forget it!

- Williamsburg is, of course, the birthplace (on the 30th of May 1765) of the American Revolution, the world's first continuing revolution, which continues to this day. Remember that, too.

21

- Yorktown is where, in what even secular historians have called a miracle, the combined American and French armies compelled the British surrender which assured not merely the independence of the United States, but more importantly the preservation of American-style democracy and the permanence of American revolutionary ideals. In a darkened world, the beacon was lit.

What happened here matters **now**, profoundly, and I try to make it clear at the beginning.

* * *

Occasionally, I have used little "teasers" to enhance a group's attention; promising, for example, that if they behave themselves, at the end of the tour I'll give them a glimpse into the future; or, as I did for a while, promising to tell them all about my nose. We'll get to the glimpse, and to the nose.

When the introduction is done and the walking begins, I know I've got 'em where I want 'em when I hear behind me "This guy is cool (or) This is gonna be fun (or) This guy is weird." Or as an adult remarked: "*This* should be interesting."

* * *

A very clear distinction must be made between Jamestown Settlement and Jamestown Island, the actual historic site administered by the National Park Service, Preservation Virginia and Colonial Williamsburg. Likewise, a very clear distinction must be made between the Yorktown Victory Center and the Yorktown Visitor Center and battlefield administered by the National Park Service.

MPAs and others at our museums not only try to make these distinctions clear, but also *urge* visitors to go to the island and go to the battlefield. To come to the Historic Triangle and not go to those places is so wrong.

The prime attractions on the island are the church built over the exposed foundations of the second church at Jamestown where the first representative assembly in Virginia met in 1619, the adjacent ongoing archaeological excavation of the original fort site discovered in 1994, and the nearby excellent new museum displaying some of the best of the approximately two million artifacts unearthed to date.

For many years, almost everyone who had an opinion on the subject opined that the fort site had eroded into the James River long ago and therefore could never be found. I disagreed, reasoning that the new church probably would have been built very near the consecrated ground of the old church and almost certainly would have been built within the immediate protection of the fort; so on several occasions with friends, I stood at the entrance of the historic church, pointed to the ground in front of the church and said that the fort would someday be found right there. When the discovery of the fort site was announced by Bill Kelso and his team of archaeologists in 1994, I was very proud of my former down-the-street neighbor (who at the time was a high school football coach), but not surprised by his magnificent discovery. It made sense.

Timely footnote: During the recent "government shutdown" (since that is what people are politely calling it), an out-of-state school group arrived for a tour at the Settlement after trying to visit the island but being stopped by barricades. (This was a day after the aging veterans, some in wheelchairs, had ignored the attempt to block access to the World War II memorial in Washington – and several days after the Carrot Tree restaurant in Yorktown had defied its National Park Service landlord and reopened to host a 100th birthday party for a special customer, then stayed open.) At the end of the tour, the teacher, who *really* wanted her youngsters to experience the island, only half-jokingly invited me to lead her group in storming the barricades. I quite reluctantly but firmly declined, saying: "B must choose his battles carefully." The time and the place just weren't right, however just the cause and delightful the thought.

* * *

Once upon a time, long ago, I would not have objected if someone said something unfavorable about Jamestown Festival Park. I certainly would never have thought that someday a slur against Jamestown Settlement would make my blood boil.

That day came a few years ago when a magazine writer rather snobbishly referred to the Settlement as the *faux* Jamestown, with all of the negative shades of meaning the word *faux* implies – like clever fakery, or fraud, or deliberate misrepresentation, or inferior quality. No, our museum is not the *real* Jamestown. Neither is it *faux*. It is *realistic*, and I cannot stress enough my admiration of the constant effort made to assure and advance the historical integrity of our programs and sites.

It has also made me unhappy to read an anonymous Internet reference to the Settlement as "a state-run tourist trap," and a similarly ignorant comment that there is nothing at the Settlement to interest anyone over the age of 13. But since so many hundreds of thousands of pleased visitors annually disprove these absurd criticisms, I shall stop venting my anger, and proceed.

SOME USEFUL DATA

To place in proper context my very small role in the daily drama of the Jamestown-Yorktown

25

Foundation, consider:

- The Foundation is ably administered by a 41-member board of trustees, supported by a private fund-raising organization with a 22-member board of directors. The current annual operating budget is $15.4 million.

- The Foundation employs 162 people full-time and more than 250 part-time, and enjoys the priceless benefits of upwards of a thousand volunteers contributing more than 61,000 hours annually. Plus: During the last fiscal year, 2,998 donors (including many employees and volunteers) contributed money to support our programs.

- During 2013, paid visitation at the two museums totaled 560,072, including 401,455 at Jamestown and 158,617 at Yorktown. (These numbers peaked in 2007, exceeding the spectacular success of the 1957 observance. In '07, paid visitation totaled 1,020,783, including 767,640 at Jamestown and 253,143 at Yorktown.) It's worth noting that residents of the Historic Triangle – James City County, Williamsburg and York County – don't have to pay an admission fee, nor do children under six. Free visitation in 2013 was at least 57,461.

- During the 2013-14 academic year, through on-site and outreach programs, our museums served 286,119 students from throughout Virginia and the nation, including 88,266 youngsters in their own classrooms in 105 Virginia school districts. Additionally, our website www.historyisfun.org provides educational services and curriculum materials for teachers and students as well as general information. In 2013, there were 1,247,249 visits to our website.

SPACE?!

While I was doing 90-minute outside tours for Visitor Services, Anne Price-Hardister and Karen Norako summoned me into Karen's office. Their mood was serious. Not a good sign.

A visitor had written on a comment card that I had "trashed NASA," so Anne and Karen were understandably curious to know: (1) Why was I trashing NASA? and (2) What does NASA have to do with Jamestown?

In answer to the first question, I said that I wasn't "trashing" NASA, but was merely pointing out what is common knowledge, that NASA is a frail shadow of its former self and that future advanced space development must depend on the private sector; and besides, I said, I made that remark only in response to a visitor's question after

I had already made my main point regarding space. In answer to the second question, I said: "Nothing."

Then what does *space* have to do with Jamestown? Good question!

I answered it well enough that Anne and Karen saw the connection, and approved my continued use of the reference.

You'll find the answer when I go to the fort, into the church.

Jamestown-Yorktown Foundation
Jamestown Settlement

*It is difficult to say what is impossible,
for the dream of yesterday is the hope of today
and the reality of tomorrow.*
Robert Goddard

CHAPTER 2: JAMESTOWN SETTLEMENT

THE PLACE

In 1957, to help the nation observe the 350th anniversary of the settlement of Jamestown Island, the Commonwealth of Virginia opened the "living history" museum Jamestown Festival Park on 37 acres of former farmland adjacent to Colonial National Historical Park. The island is less than a mile from the museum, and can be seen from our pier into the James River.

The original museum included an administrative building, a separate cafeteria and an indoor gallery of exhibits, plus the outdoor sites – the Indian village, the three replica ships and the fort. The first thing built on the site was the Discovery Tower on the great lawn. It stands today, symbolizing the mast of a ship and the steady progress of humanity through the ages (the latter an almost forgotten aspect of its designer's original intent).

In 1990, Jamestown Festival Park was renamed Jamestown Settlement.

Anticipating 2007, a decade in advance Virginia began a total transformation of the Settlement, tearing down the three original buildings in phases and replacing them with the grand facility the visitor sees today. When I became an MPA in 1999, only the administration building was gone, and the new education section was still under construction. Thus, I had the interesting experience not only of witnessing the transformation, but also of enduring the inconveniences it often caused. (This construction program included not only the main building, but also a Central Support Facility midway the museums, a new Powhatan village based on recent archaeology, a new Godspeed and Discovery – a total investment of almost $100 million.)

The property itself has some historical significance; but then, every inch of ground in the Tidewater of Virginia has some story to tell. Archaeology informs us that a wooded area between the village and the fort was used for hundreds of years as an Indian hunting campground, and that there was a farmhouse in the 1640s (fronting on the Great Road) very near our Discovery Tower. Neither site is identified for the visiting public, but should be. Archaeology makes history immediately near, not vaguely distant. People love archaeology.

The Great Road crossed this property. In 1676, a loyalist army of more than a thousand men moved along that road to attack Nathaniel Bacon's rebels on the island. In 1781, British and French troops skirmished here. There should be signage near our front doors telling visitors how close they are to this history.

THE LOOP

For MPAs and the groups arriving on buses, the action begins on the loop, where on busy days the constant coming and going of scores of buses and thousands of visiting children and adults demands a degree of cooperation *and* enthusiasm I have experienced at a workplace only once before (the year I spent as a manual laborer in the greenhouses of the old Williamsburg Pottery).

Thank goodness, there's a Plan, and competent people to make it work. Otherwise, chaos would prevail; sometimes, it seems to prevail even with a Plan.

The loop is a great place for MPA socializing, getting to know one another better, passing along the latest news and information (a lot of it having to do with history), talking about current events – with the constant understanding and awareness that the conversation must end the instant one's group arrives.

Whenever I board a bus, the first thing I do is shake the driver's hand and thank him or her for bringing my people safely. "Without you," I say, "I wouldn't have a job." Then, usually with a microphone (which even on a $500,000 heavily computerized bus sometimes doesn't work quite right), I greet the people and state the rules – no backpacks unless carried by an adult, no beverages except water, no chewing gum. Each of these rules has a common-sense reason.

The bus drivers are professionals, too, admirably competent not only in driving those machines on the open highway and in dense urban traffic, but also in dealing with people of all sorts from all kinds of places. It's always fun just to sit and chat with the drivers. They have great stories to tell, from all across the land. (I drove a school bus for a couple of years when I was in college, so I have a natural yearning to drive one of these modern buses – but just around the loop on a *very* slow day, *very* slowly.)

THE GALLERY

With students especially but also with adults, you notice it as soon as a group begins entering the grand hallway – a hush, as in a library, or a church. MPA buddy Don Swain explained it best: "Adults demonstrate to kids a respect for history in a lot of ways. This building shows them we have put our money where our mouth is."

There is much to see in the gallery, so much that on a guided tour I can stop and talk at relatively few exhibits. The gallery is best experienced at leisure.

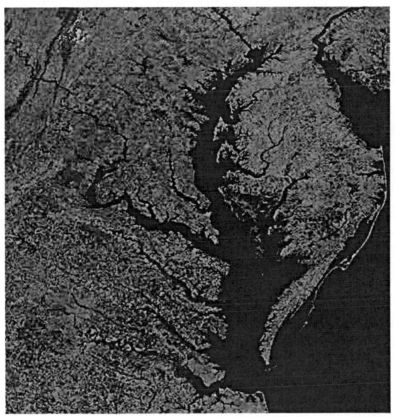

NASA

Region of the Chesapeake Bay

* * *

I think the study of the history of a place should begin with its geography, which more often than not heavily influences its history. A perfect example of this is Virginia. (Geography studies are increasingly neglected and even ignored in our schools. I think this trend is stupid and in today's world dangerous, bordering on criminal negligence. Young people enjoy geography well taught. Teach 'em!)

Immediately after entering the gallery, I stop my groups in front of a satellite photograph of where we are on the planet, in the Tidewater of Virginia. I point to the Baltimore area, to Washington, to Richmond, then to a large dark area, and ask: "What's this?" Almost everybody knows it's the Atlantic Ocean; a few youngsters (in groups from California and Louisiana) have identified it as our other ocean, the Pacific.

Then I point to a smaller dark area and ask: "What's this?" A few say it's a river; most who respond know it's the Chesapeake Bay. "Chesapeake" in the Algonquian language means "big water" – and it is. In fact, it is the largest natural harbor in the world. You can put all of the ships and boats in the world in our Chesapeake Bay, and they would fill only a small fraction of it; it is **huge**. Ships can pass on the bay in daylight and not see one another.

Into the Chesapeake flow many rivers, the glory of Virginia. According to the History Channel, some 150 rivers (beginning up in New York and

Pennsylvania) flow into the bay. In Virginia, the most notable are the James, the York, the Rappahannock and the Potomac, not forgetting the Matta and the Po and the Ni which form the Mattaponi which merges with the Pamunkey to form the York, or the Elizabeth, the Lafayette and others I cannot recall at the moment – and not even mentioning the Meherrin, the Blackwater and the Nottoway, which flow southward into Albemarle Sound in North Carolina.

So is this a good place to hunt, fish, farm, raise a family? Yes! (John Smith said it best: "Heaven and earth never combined better to frame a place for man's habitation.")

And did the people living here 400 years ago have a good transportation system? The best in the world – the rivers! You can go from Richmond to Philadelphia and never touch land, or stop anywhere in between. In such a region 400 years ago, the importance of the canoe cannot be overstated.

People had been living in this region for at least 16,000 years before the Europeans and Africans began arriving. Archaeologists have found artifacts that old at the Cactus Hill site, on the upper Nottoway; artifacts found on Jamestown Island date back 10,000 years.

At the time of the voyages of Columbus, the Algonquin people occupied this coastal plain of Virginia, with Sioux to the west and Iroquois to the south. The Algonquins called their homeland

35

Tsenecommacah, the "densely inhabited land," their spiritual center being Werowocomoco on the Pamunkey (now the York) River.

One historian has estimated the Algonquin population in Virginia at the time of Columbus at 170,000 "and perhaps many more"; when the English arrived, the Algonquins numbered very approximately 15,000. Trade relations between tribes of the Algonquin, Sioux and Iroquois were sometimes disrupted by warfare, contributing to the tensions, politics and diplomacy here in the early 17th century.

Ships of several European nations were exploring in the Chesapeake within a few years of the "discovery" of what became known as the Americas. Spain claimed this region, which became (like everything else north of Florida) North Florida. The Spanish made two attempts to establish a permanent presence in the region, but failed – and that is another remarkable story deserving to be better known.

The Englishmen entering the Chesapeake Bay in 1607 had to hope that the native people would permit them to stay and not kill them, and had to pray they would be ready when the seemingly inevitable Spanish attack came.

* * *

Across the room is an exhibit noting the sources of our information about this time in history – words written by the English and pictures drawn by the English (there being no written language or representational art among the Powhatans), artifacts in museums and private collections and artifacts unearthed by archaeologists. These sources are so obvious to most groups that I could in good pedagogical conscience walk past them without stopping.

But I stop, because here also is a cross-section of a 600-year-old cypress tree, with an important story to tell – and that story is only part of a longer, larger story I shall now tell.

The Road to Nowhere

Prelude

About 50 miles directly south of Jamestown Island is the town of Courtland (formerly Jerusalem) in Southampton County, long the homeland of my father's people.

In my youth, we were a Navy family – my father and two uncles and an aunt were in the Navy – so my grandparents' modest home along the Old Bridge Road, near the highway into Courtland, was a special place to me and my cousins, a home port of sorts. Often, we went down the two-mile dirt road to where the Cypress Bridge once crossed a lazy swampy section of the Nottoway River snaking through the countryside.

The bridge was dismantled in the 1940s. I remember being in a car driving across it, and can still hear the creaking. The pilings of that bridge still stand. Alongside them, at low water, you can see the wooden stubs of the pilings of an earlier bridge – as I learned later, the one in use at the time of the Southampton Slave Insurrection of 1831.

Even in my youth, I "knew" about the local uprising; an historical marker on the highway at the entrance to our road spoke briefly of it. And I "knew" about Nat Turner, the leader of the uprising; the adults sometimes made reference to him. Basically, I "knew" nothing. But I was aware.

To me and my cousins, that wonderful road went nowhere.

Did it really go nowhere? The real story:

Part 1

That dirt road and that older bridge are on the 1830 map on the cover of my book **Tomorrow Jerusalem: The Story of Nat Turner and the Southampton Slave Insurrection of 1831.**

Nat and his men, repulsed in what would become known as the Battle at Parker's Field near Jerusalem, attempted a flanking movement, riding toward the Cypress Bridge downriver, but found it too strongly defended. Thus, the path of the insurrection was diverted.

Whatever its course, the uprising would have been suppressed soon. But if that bridge had not been so strongly defended, the ending to the story of what happened in rural Southampton – and the extent of its impact on history – would have been very different. I might not be here today, writing this.

Part 2

The Starving Time at Jamestown, the winter of 1609-10, was as terrible as its name suggests. Besieged by the Powhatans, the island's population shrank from about 300 to about 60. Most of the colonists starved to death; and yes, there were instances of cannibalism.

But the problem wasn't just the Powhatans, and it wasn't just during that winter. Off and on for about 20 years, hunger plagued the early settlers, the need for food (particularly corn) affecting trade relations and occasionally leading to fighting with the Powhatans, who sometimes didn't seem to have enough food for themselves.

In 1624, the biggest battle ever fought between the Powhatans and the English, about 600 Powhatans defending their growing fields of corn from about 60 English, raged for two days, until a small group of colonists moved behind the natives and cut down their growing corn, disheartening the Powhatans, who knew their families would go hungry that winter.

When I became an MPA, I assumed, like most people assumed, that those early English were, well, how shall I put it nicely, at best incompetent, at worst just plain lazy. Remember that John Smith was compelled to decree: "He who will not work shall not eat." Lazy, right?

Wrong! A few years after I became an MPA, dendrologists (tree scientists) went to the end of the road to nowhere and by studying the tree rings of cypress trees 600-800 years old made a major, some might say startling, discovery – that the English arrived at Jamestown in 1607 during the worst drought in this region in 800 years, and that it lasted off and on for about 20 years.

This new knowledge, combined with the increasing evidence of busyness being unearthed on the island, fundamentally changes a key aspect of our previous perception of those English, and those Powhatans.

Part 3

According to the English, the Powhatans had canoes (each canoe made from a single cypress tree) big enough to hold 40 or more men. Imagine the size of the tree required – not only old and tall but also wide, so men could sit side by side.

Now, either the English exaggerated or the question arises: Do we have any such big cypress trees in Virginia today? When I became an MPA, very familiar with the cypress trees of my youth down there at the end of the road to nowhere, I said: No.

Today, I say: Yes! Because in 2005, retired Virginia Tech dendrologist Bryan Carmean went to the end of the Old Bridge Road, put his canoe in the water, and nearby began discovering what proved to be 37 acres of awesome cypress (and tupelo) trees, some dating back about 2,000 years. The recently deceased matriarch, Big Mama, at the time of its discovery the biggest and oldest bald cypress known

John Bryant

Bryant kinsmen assembled at the base of Big Mama

41

in North America, stands 123 feet high. Our Discovery Tower is 80 feet high.

In recent years of exploring the remoter riverine nooks and crannies of the Tidewater, Bryan has found even older and bigger cypress trees. (His original great discovery is now the core of the new 380-acre Cypress Bridge Swamp Natural Area Preserve, down the road from the Big Mama Memorial Wastewater Treatment Plant.)

John Bryant & Michael Bryant

Bryant kinsmen on the menu at the base of Big Mama

Part 4

The 1677 Treaty of Middle Plantation bringing peace between the English and the surviving tribes of the Tidewater granted permanent land north of the James to the Pamunkey and Mattaponi tribes and south of the James to the Nottoway tribe.

The latter people, and their river, had become known to the encroaching English as the Nottoway because the Powhatans called them and/or their river the Nadawa, the Algonquian word for snake.

On trips into Courtland in my youth, my elders would direct my attention to a certain old fellow often seen in town and remind me: That's the last of the Nottoways; when he's gone, they're all gone. This did not mean much to me at the time, but I duly, somewhat sadly noted it.

Well, the old fellow is long gone. So are they all gone? No. Many years ago, to resist racist state policies aimed at Indians as well as blacks, the Nottoways went into stealth mode, hiding their tribal identity except among themselves, doing it so well that eventually other people believed that the fellow in town was, in fact, the last of the Nottoways. Early in the last decade, they re-emerged as the Cheronenhaka people of the Iroquois nation, hundreds of them in two tribal divisions, flaunting their native identity, holding annual pow wows – the program for one pow wow devoting a page to "The Last of the Nottoways," with a good picture of the man. This story became even better when the Cheroenhaka/Nottoway purchased 100 acres in Southampton to re-establish, symbolically and spiritually, what might be the homeland of the

43

most ancient people in Virginia. They have named their new town Cattashowrock.

Question: Where, exactly, is Cattashowrock? Think hard now. Clue: Along the road to . . .

* * *

Back to the tour.

A statue of Wahunsonacock, commonly known as the Powhatan, or Chief Powhatan, dominates the next area where I like to stop. I didn't have an opinion of him one way or another when I became an MPA; now, he is a hero of mine.

Decades before the English landed at what would become Jamestown, Spanish germs (particularly smallpox) had traveled into the Chesapeake region along the Indian trade routes. Thrice, according to Wahunsonacock, great deaths had ravaged the people of Tsenecommacah – and the Spanish themselves had come on several troublesome occasions.

At a time of crisis to his people, Wahunsonacock arose as their great leader.

Inheriting six tribes (including the Powhatan) from his mother, he employed warfare, marriage and other forms of diplomacy to become the dominant werowance (chief) of about 36 tribes of Algonquian-speaking people in a region ranging from just below the Potomac near Washington to south of the James, from Richmond to the Atlantic. Among the Algonquins of the Tidewater, only the powerful Chickahominy (whose distinctive form of democracy endures to this day) remained fully independent, but they, too, were disposed to cooperate against a common enemy.

Wahunsonacock was well aware of the dangers posed by the Europeans, especially the Spanish, but reasoned that the English might become allies of the Powhatan in fighting the Spanish. Thus, he was open to the idea of an English presence, unlike his younger brother Opechancanough, who reportedly never liked the idea.

Wahunsonacock had numerous wives and children. His favorite child was Pocahontas. Did her love her? Yes, possibly too much. When he learned of her death, it broke his heart and spirit; within a year, he became too weak to be werowance and was replaced by two of his brothers, and died.

Which brings us to Pocahontas. Are you ready for the truth about Pocahontas? Can you handle it? Are you sure?

* * *

I divert my group's attention away from the nearby scenes from the cartoon "Pocahontas" and direct it to our copy of the 18th century painting of the "real" Pocahontas based on a 17th century etching done while she was in England. Her hair is styled and she is clothed in the English manner. She does not look very Powhatan. Whatever, this is as close as we can get to seeing her as she was.

Truth time.

I ask my students (and adults) how many of them have seen the cartoon film. Most have.

Was that film accurate and truthful and honest? No, most know by now.

For the record: We have no talking trees in Virginia, no singing rivers. If a raccoon comes near B, no matter what language it's speaking, what does B do? Some suggest: Shoot him. No, I reply, B doesn't pack heat; B *runs*, B says: Legs, do your thing! Whatever Disney suggests, I say: Beware any approaching raccoon, even if it's trying to strike up a conversation! The critter is probably rabid. (Also, since we're setting the record straight here: If I walk through a waterfall in 1608 with my gun in front of me, I am a complete idiot – the water's going to put out the fire my gun needs to go boom – and my mama didn't raise a *complete* idiot.)

How old was Pocahontas when John Smith was in Virginia? Forget about Disney. She was probably 10, 11, 12 years old.

Was there any "romance" between her and John Smith? No. Nobody ever said there was. It's fiction, and it began long before Hollywood.

Did she save John Smith's life? Probably not. We now have reason to believe – and Smith might or might not have realized it at the time – that the celebrated 1607 ceremony at Werowocomoco at which Pocahontas supposedly saved Smith was a standard Algonquin ceremony of initiation, involving symbolic death and symbolic rebirth; and there is reason to suspect that as a child, even as the daughter of the paramount chief, Pocahontas would not have been present.

So what *did* she do to make herself one of the most influential people who ever lived – and a genuine heroine to me?

I am fortunate to live on the Hickory Sign Post Road, an old, narrow, winding mile-long road with a one-lane bridge across a swampy area. It's a very minor road in the elaborate transportation system of the community today, but until less than a century ago it was still the main road between Jamestown and Williamsburg and the world beyond – thus, probably, the most significant surviving segment of the Great Road and the earlier Powhatan footpath across the peninsula between the James and York rivers. When I look out my front window at that road, I imagine things, like a slow convoy of Model-T Fords coming from the ferry, or Union and Confederate troops on the march, or British and French and Continental soldiers, or Washington and Jefferson and Henry riding by, or . . . But I digress.

When the great Powhatan sent his people across this peninsula to deal with the English, who accompanied them along that path in front of my house? Pocahontas – which sent a deliberate message: The ruler of this land was entrusting to the English the life of his most precious child, a supreme act of goodwill and peaceful intention. Thus, the child became a symbol of peace – and hope – to the newcomers.

She was no ordinary child, not by the standards of the 17th century, certainly not by today's standards. She was far more mature in her thinking and sense of responsibility than today's youngsters, the product of a Powhatan culture in which girls could be married at 13 and boys at 15 and all of them were expected to behave like adults. She was very lively, very bright. She was a truly remarkable young girl who became a truly remarkable young woman.

In the years following Smith's abrupt departure from Virginia, Pocahontas married a Powhatan man named Kokoum, and with him had a child named Kokoum. Her husband was killed in a clash with the English, and she was later basically kidnapped to be used as leverage in bargaining with her father.

Wahunsonacock, to his great credit, rejected any deal.

Living among the English, but never personally losing her identity as a Powhatan, Pocahontas eventually professed herself a Christian and, acquiring the name Rebecca, married planter John Rolfe in a church ceremony considered important to both cultures and with Powhatans as well as English in attendance. Together, the Rolfes would have a son, Thomas.

I have skipped past a vital moment in Virginia, American and world history.

At the time Pocahontas uttered the words saying she would marry John Rolfe, the Powhatans and the English were at war and on the eve of a great battle. The instant Pocahontas spoke those words, the war ended, and for eight critical years the English in Virginia and the Powhatans in Tsenecommacah enjoyed what became known as the Pocahontas Peace.

I have often said half-jokingly that if Pocahontas were alive today and running for president I would not only vote for her but also go out and raise money for her campaign (which as anyone who knows me knows is a radical departure from my custom). But note: I say it only *half*-jokingly.

Footnote 1: In restored Williamsburg is the handsome home of Peyton Randolph, unanimously elected first president of the Continental Congress in 1774, first leader of the united Americans, called by some people at the time the Father of His Country – mostly unknown now, the greatest forgotten hero of the Revolution . . . and a proud descendant of Pocahontas.

Footnote 2: One day with a group of eighth-graders from California, after I had finished "critiquing" the Disney version of events, a girl raised her hand and smilingly said with soft pride:

"My father was the director of that film." *Awkward moment.* In front of her classmates, I hastened to assure her that I was sure the film was very well directed, that as a cartoon it was really good, but . . . well, it still wasn't accurate history. I think she understood.

* * *

Two statues, and a popular light display, dominate the next-to-last gallery area I particularly like to visit.

Njinga

One statue is of Njinga, the warrior queen of Kongo Angola in western Africa.

Before the English arrived at Jamestown, the Spanish and the Portuguese had already taken more than a million Africans into slavery in the Americas, many of them exported from or through Njinga's homeland. Off and on for more than 30 years, Njinga led her people in resisting the Portuguese.

Did she know how to read and write? No, most people instinctively reply.

In fact, she was one of the best educated women in the world, literate not only in her own language, but also in Portuguese and Latin.

* * *

The first recorded instance of Africans arriving in Virginia was in 1619, when 20-plus men and women were exchanged for provisions by the English privateer which had captured a Portuguese shipload of slaves (victims of civil war in Kongo Angola) originally destined for the Spanish Caribbean.

Here against their will, with no real hope of ever seeing their homeland again, ignorant of the language and customs of the white people and probably expecting the worst, nonetheless the 20-plus (as well as other Africans arriving in limited numbers in those early years) were much more fortunate than the ones who remained on that captured ship.

At the time, slavery did not legally exist in Virginia. Therefore, we have good reason to believe that the early Africans basically shared the labor status of most of the arriving whites and served some form of indenture. This notion is supported by recorded instances of certain Africans who served in the militia, owned property, voted in elections.

However, the constant need for more and more labor to grow more and more tobacco to make more and more money for the settlers and for England meant that by the middle of the 17th century slavery had become legal and ever more tightly defined and regulated, with fewer rights and opportunities for free blacks.

Opechancanough

The other statue is of Opechancanough, the greatest of the Powhatan warriors, in historic stature comparable (in my opinion) to the later and far better known Sitting Bull, Tecumseh, Geronimo, Cochise, Red Cloud, Osceola.

Opechancanough was a warchief in all three Anglo-Powhatan wars, his resistance ending only in 1646 when he was an invalid prisoner on Jamestown Island and one of his jailers shot him in the back – a cowardly act, the English called it, because they did respect the old chief (more than 90 years old when he died) and returned his body to his people for proper burial.

Opechancanough has descendants living among us. Can we get along with them? Sure, almost everyone says. Indeed, I say, one of our best teachers at this museum is Samuel Opechancanough McGowan, and Sam's mother has served on our board of trustees!

Research Assignment – Enjoy some quality time learning the story of Paquiquineo, the Algonquin lad who (voluntarily or otherwise) boarded a Spanish ship in the lower Chesapeake region in 1561 and spent nine years living and learning in Spain, Mexico and Cuba, then came home in 1570 as Don Luis de Velasco (namesake of the Viceroy of New Spain), escorting eight Jesuits seeking to establish a mission to convert the natives.

Don Luis led them overland from somewhere near present-day Jamestown to somewhere along the York River, where he abandoned them and returned to his people, then directed the killing of the Jesuits.

Some have speculated that Don Luis might have been Opechancanough; others, that he might have been Wahunsonacock. If not, he was certainly a contemporary of those men, and his experience among the Spanish probably influenced subsequent Algonquin attitudes and actions toward the Spanish, and the English, and he might even have been present during early contact with the latter. Whoever he was and whatever his later influence, he played a critical role in history; by ending the Spanish mission, he erased the prospect of a permanent early Spanish settlement in the Chesapeake.

Footnote: A fine student of mine at Walsingham Academy many years ago – Monsignor Russell Smith, S.J. – has been leading the effort to have the eight Jesuits declared saints, as martyrs to the faith.

* * *

With some appropriate groups, to stress the ideal of honest reconciliation, I note that Nat Turner has descendants living among us, and that a distant uncle of mine was Nat's jailer, and I ask: Can I get along with Nat Turner's descendants? Sometimes, there is doubt. In fact, a dear friend of mine is Bruce

Turner, a high-level computer consultant in Virginia Beach and Nat's great-great-great grandson. I have become acquainted with numerous members of the Turner family. Good people.

Some years ago, the Hatfields and the McCoys signed a so-called peace treaty. Their celebrated family feud had no apparent influence on the course of history, but its ending was widely publicized. In contrast, almost no one (with the commendable exception of WHRO public television) has reported the infinitely more meaningful reconciliation represented by the friendship of Bruce Turner and Richard Lincoln Francis, the Clerk of Court in Southampton. Rick's family suffered the greatest loss during the uprising led by Bruce's ancestor. Today, these fine men cooperate to preserve and convey the memory of what happened in 1831. (Incidentally, Rick happens to be a nephew of Abraham Lincoln, and is very proud of it.)

* * *

Oh yeah, I almost forgot – the light display, a large plain map of the Tidewater of Virginia with three simple buttons to illuminate the dramatic expansion of English settlement.

With a school group, I appoint three students as Button-Pusher Number 1, Number 2 and Number 3. They come forward. I ask if they are ready –

especially Button-Pusher Number 3, because that display is *really* dramatic. They say they are ready.

I ask: What's the first thing you do, after unpacking, when you move into a new neighborhood? You check it out. You begin meeting people. "You make friends," many youngsters reply. (To some folks, finding the nearest 7-Eleven is a high priority.)

Well, that's basically what the English did during their first year in Virginia, exploring, drawing maps, making contact with the tribes.

Hit it, Number 1

Red lights scattered throughout the Tidewater indicate the location of the major Powhatan villages as of 1608, all located along waterways.

As previously noted, the Algonquins numbered approximately 15,000.

Hit it, Number 2

Blue lights concentrated along the James indicate English settlements as of 1625 – more than a thousand newcomers now, the number steadily increasing despite the high mortality rate.

Of the 104 men who landed at Jamestown in May of 1607, 66 were dead by December. Of the first 8,000 or so who came in the early years, 6,000 didn't survive the first year.

On a single day in 1622 – March 22, a date annually memorialized in Virginia churches for more than a century to come – the population went from about 1,250 at sunrise to about 850 at sunset, because of a concerted Powhatan attack along the James which in addition to killing so many colonists "broke the hearts of all the rest," a survivor noted.

This was not always a safe and pleasant place to be, and that is well worth remembering.

The Powhatans, it should be noted, were still in charge in most of Tsenecommacah-Virginia.

Then, two things happened.

OK . . . Hit it, Number 3

Wow!

Blue lights are everywhere in the Tidewater of 1675. A few red lights remain. The English (and a whole lot of other people from other places) now number approximately 50,000; the Powhatans, perhaps 3,000.

The two things (besides warfare and hunger) that happened were:

(1) The newcomers kept coming, and they kept coming, and they kept coming, and I could keep this up all day because even today they keep coming, and they keep coming, and . . . Reportedly, a majority of the people now living in Virginia were not born in Virginia.

(2) English germs finished the job that the Spanish germs had begun. By century's end, the population of newcomers was about 90,000; of the Powhatans, about a thousand. From the native perspective, the coming of the English was a great tragedy. (One historian has roughly estimated that Earth's population in 1491 was about 500 million, about 100 million of them in the Americas. It is generally accepted that European diseases eradicated about 90 percent of the native people in this hemisphere. Whatever the precise numbers, you can do the basic math for yourself.)

* * *

When appropriate, I usher a group into a small theatre to watch a brief film about the origins of representative government in America, focusing on the initial session of the Virginia General Assembly during the summer of 1619 – to my mind an event more important than that of 1607.

After the viewing, I huddle the group outside the theatre, noting that if you were born poor and illiterate in England in 1619 you were probably going to remain that way for the rest of your life, with little or no opportunity to learn even the rudiments of reading and writing and reckoning numbers, or to acquire property and the better things of life, or to become eligible to vote, or to serve on a local governing council, much less in Parliament. Virtually unthinkable.

In Virginia, quickly, the rigid thinking and strict social and economic caste systems of English life changed radically. Here, the value and dignity of the individual – and the opportunities available to a hard-working individual teamed with others – sharply increased. What mattered most here was not so much your social standing back in England as your usefulness in helping us to survive and prosper.

Being 3,000 or so miles and two or so months away from the comforts (and authority) of England, and surrounded by uncertainty here, made the early Virginians – most of whom came here with nothing as mere indentured servants – uncommonly enterprising and egalitarian, and very independent-minded. Twice in the 17th century, the Virginians forced – peacefully – the ouster of royal governors.

I conclude a visit to the gallery with a factoid which startled me a bit when I learned it: At one point in the latter 17th century, a majority of the members of the Virginia Assembly were former indentured servants!

Diane Smith
The Discovery Tower

THE VILLAGE

In contrast to the busier and noisier activities at the ships and in the fort, the village is normally a more quiet and serene place.

Our village, or town, consists of five yehakins (homes) with outside cooking areas, deer hides stretched stiff so visitors can use oyster shells to scrape the fur off preparatory to tanning and softening the hide for clothing, a tree trunk being made into a canoe, work stations for pottery, cordage, tool-making, a display of trade items for and from the English.

I prefer that a visit to the village begin in a yehakin, so if possible I head directly toward my favorite, and, if it's empty, I fill it. (Alice Roosevelt Longsworth, Teddy's feisty daughter, in her later years stated her philosophy of life thusly: "Fill what's empty, empty what's full, and scratch where it itches." Not relevant, but funny, and quaintly wise.)

* * *

As a group slowly files into a yehakin – beholding the strange and delightful array of deerskin-covered beds, the sloping walls displaying fishing nets and spears and the furs of various animals, the small firepit on the earthen floor, the baskets for dried food hanging from the ceiling – a certain question is often asked: "Is everything in here real?" I answer (with appropriate gestures): "Everything in here is real – except me. I am an android. This is to make certain that your tour is perfect, tour is perfect, tour is perfect . . . " This doesn't get as many laughs as it should, but the laughs it does get are loud and hearty, which is admittedly very pleasing to the ear, to the ear, to . . .

The yehakin is a fabulous classroom, once my students and/or adults are seated on the beds and/or standing in such a way that all can see and hear me, and these are some of my favorite teaching points:

Lesson 1

Are Powhatans Indians? Are Apaches Indians? How about Cherokees? Eskimos? Aztecs?

Most people, young and old, routinely say yes; some people hesitate about the Eskimos and Aztecs; a few people, the older ones mostly, say no, such people are Native Americans. "I'm a native American," I note, "and I don't have a drop of indigenous blood in me, that I know of. So I'm not accepting that answer."

The simple fact is that when Columbus "discovered" the "New World" in 1492, he didn't really know (and never did realize) where he was. He thought he had reached Asia and called the people Indians, and we are stuck with that word. It is bogus.

About 20 miles from here live the Mattaponi people. What do the **Mattaponi** like to be called? . . . Aha . . . What does an Apache like to be called?

A Cherokee?

An Aztec?

An Eskimo (not to be confused with an Inuit or an Athabascan)?

Et cetera!

Call 'em who they are, and they'll appreciate it.

A school group from Tuscaloosa, Alabama, does **not** want to be identified as coming from Auburn, Alabama; that's not their tribe. And in the same sense, South Carolinians and North Carolinians do **not** care to have their IDs lumped together.

A person who is a Tuscaloosa Alabama American compares to someone who is a Pamunkey Powhatan Algonquin – local, regional and national tribes. A class can have a tribal identity, a school, a neighborhood, a church – a strong sense of self and of community, distinct and special, and proud.

Speaking of tribes, one day I had a great group of wide-eyed youngsters from the Southwest, from a half-dozen or so reservation tribes, including (as I recall) Apache, Navajo and Hopi. I asked them to speak some in their native languages, and they did. I couldn't understand a word they said, but I was enthralled. I could have stood there all day, listening to the music of their voices, the heritage of their people.

Lesson 2

In the village, in a yehakin, I ask if any of the students can speak at least a few words in a language other than English. There are always several students who can and then do, at least a few words. An increasing number of groups, reflecting the dynamic changing demographics of America, are predominantly students to whom English is a second (or even third) language, often still a new one. Sometimes, I ask a native speaker of a particularly interesting language to speak to us in that language.

Then I ask the students how many of them speak at least a few words in Algonquian, the language of the Powhatan people, which leads to a discussion of some of the common English words derived from Algonquin – like skunk, chipmunk, opossum, raccoon, muskrat, persimmon, pecan (its pronunciation being a matter of considerable regional dispute), chinquapin, wigwam, tomahawk, moccasins, pone, hominy, succotash – words which began entering our vocabulary when the English went around asking: "Kaka torowines yowo?" What do you call this?

And no, for the thousandth time, the greeting "How" is not an Algonquian word. It's Lakota Sioux.

Lesson 3

What do all of these furs tell you about the man of the family? That he's a good hunter.

What do they tell you about the woman of the family? That she's a good decorator. Never doubt that the Powhatans appreciated beauty, in many forms. In any culture at any time, flowers are flowers, sunrises and sunsets are sunrises and sunsets, a rainbow is wondrous, and (especially in

Virginia) autumn leaves are dazzling. If anything, our village is a bit too drab.

Lesson 4

Where is the kitchen? If you point to the little firepit on the ground, I note that a low fire would always be burning inside a yehakin – to protect the home from rotting away in the humid Virginia climate and to keep dry the preserved food in the hanging baskets. Then I must ask if you really want a high fire in a grass house (because sometimes you need high heat on the stove or in the oven), or if you really think you can simultaneously cook three or four things, a day's supply of cooked food, in that very small space.

The Powhatan family's cooking area was outside. Except in very bad weather, that's where the food was cooked and served. The Powhatans didn't have breakfast, lunch and dinner; they had something called "hungry." The woman would start the process of cooking, then proceed to her other chores. Family members could come to get something to eat as and when they got hungry. Simple as that.

Lesson 5

Would this yehakin survive a hurricane? Most people say no, definitely not; very few say yes.

During my experience, the score is: Yehakins 2, Hurricanes 0.

Hurricane Isabel in 2003 was especially brutal to this region, passing directly over this museum – and over my home. There were 21 trees down on my property (none on the house), 13 trees blocking the road I live on, and so much such damage to the area that for almost two days I couldn't even get to the Settlement to see what damage had been done.

Very little! With the hurricane pushing the waters of the Chesapeake Bay inland, raising the level of the James River well above even the pilings on the pier, the ships had ridden out the storm well. In the village, it seemed that not a hair was out of place, though I was later told that a section of matting on one of the yehakins had worked loose. It so happens – and older folks notice this and can guess correctly the right answer to the initial question – that the yehakins are wisely shaped like Airstream trailers! (Over on the island, the National Park Service's masonry visitor center was moved off its foundation, and had to be razed.)

Lesson 6

Here comes a question for people who can think: Keeping in mind that building this yehakin requires all of these saplings set in the ground, several acres of river reeds to make the mats to cover it, plus maybe a mile of different types of cordage to weave the mats and hold the whole place together, how *long* would it take to build this yehakin?

Think.

Doesn't it all depend on whether all of your building materials are ready and how many people are working how long and how hard to do it?

The Amish people build great elaborate barns in **one day**, which they can do because they have a plan, the necessary materials are ready, and the people – men and women, young and old – cooperate and work well together to get the job done. There is a major lesson in this.

Footnote: When a young Powhatan man and woman got married, the people of the village built their first home for them.

Pop Quiz

Explain the term "progress of humanity" by defining the following words:
(1) Civility.
(2) Communication.
(3) Conciliation.
(4) Consensus.
(5) Cooperation.
(6) Collegiality.
(7) Community.

* * *

I much prefer that one of our interpreters talk about the family cooking area and foodways and such, but I am prepared to do it alone if need be, which on busy days is often.

The Powhatans obtained most of their food (besides gathering berries and nuts and roots and such) in three ways, by:

(1) Growing it – beans and squash and corn, lots and lots of corn, the only food then available in Virginia edible 365 days of the year and thus precious, sometimes beyond price, to hungry Powhatans and English alike.

(2) Hunting for it – birds of all types, of course, but mostly four-legged creatures of all sizes, particularly the deer, not only for its abundant meat, but also for its hide to blanket the beds and make clothing, its bones and horns to make a wide variety of tools, its brain to use in softening the hide, its sinew to make cordage for various tough uses, including bowstring. In the foot of the deer is a bone shaped roughly like a fish-hook. Guess what you can make it into . . . ? . . . You guessed it! (A Pamunkey friend describes the deer as "Walmart on the hoof – one-stop shopping."

(3) Fishing for it – clams, mussels, oysters, lobsters, a great diversity of finfish. When the fishing was good, it was very good; according to the English, a man could walk across a river on the backs of the fish. And consider this: Allowed to mature, an oyster in the rivers of the Chesapeake

region could grow to the size of a large dinner plate and be a whole meal; one crab could feed four people; and a sturgeon might be 14 feet long and weigh half a ton.

During the times of drought, the crops didn't grow well, the fish didn't spawn normally, and the deer went many miles inland in search of fresh water. (Besides, there weren't as many deer in the Tidewater then as you might think. Supposedly, there are more now than there were then, and I believe it, based on the number, upwards of a dozen at a time, who routinely visit my yard. One day several years ago, with freshly fallen snow thick upon the ground, the deer began coming out of the woods behind my house, a slow but steady stream of them, until my wife and I counted 31 congregating in our front and side yards – and then six more emerged from the woods to join them – 37 deer!)

* * *

A Powhatan woman could bake, boil, broil, roast, toast and fry food. What could she *not* do that you do in your kitchen almost every day? Clue: The answer begins with "m" and ends with "icrowave." Got it?

So who was primarily responsible for cooking, the men or the women? The women, in all of their chores assisted by the children, who were attending home school every day.

Who was almost exclusively responsible for the farming, the men or the women? The women. (Only the men grew and touched the tobacco used only in spiritual ceremonies and too harsh to be smoked in the European manner.)

Who was mostly responsible for building the homes, the men or the women? The women. Keep in mind that men are gone from the village most of the time, hunting, fishing, trading, perhaps fighting.

Ah, but who *owns* the homes, the men or the women? The women.

And if you become the werowance, the chief of the tribe, is it because of who your daddy is or who your mama is? Your mama.

* * *

Having made it abundantly clear to a group that women were very important and influential in Powhatan society, I might say (assuming it's not an all-girl group): "Boys! Are you listenin' to me?" When I know I have their strict attention, I declare: "Women rule!" The responses to this declaration, among the boys and the girls and the adults, are fun to observe.

When practical, I call out to a male visitor in the vicinity: "Sir! You and I have never met, is that correct?"

He says yes, assuring us of his objectivity.

I say: "Do women rule?"

He smiles and, with his wife often standing nearby, almost invariably (with a couple of rare and humorous exceptions) replies strongly in the affirmative: "Absolutely (or) Yes (or) You bet they do!"

If his wife is nearby, I might add: "My compliments, ma'am. You've done a good job with him."

* * *

Initially, the English scorned the seemingly crudely built Powhatan canoes, thinking they looked like animal feeding troughs, which they did. Soon, the English were trading generously to obtain the obviously expertly built craft, because (1) they didn't leak, (2) they lasted a long long time, and (3) they got the job done in transporting one's self and one's stuff from one place to another.

I am frequently asked: How long did it take to build one? If you remember what we discussed inside the yehakin, you don't need my help to answer this one. Right?

Diane Smith

Carol Wiers enjoying her job

* * *

Frankly, I wouldn't mind a visit to the village with the interpreters doing *all* of the teaching, which is why on slower days I sometimes sneak in an additional interpreter to enrich my group's experience. Whether it's Lynn Powell making cordage in her gentle patient way, or John Giere talking about canoes, or Anastasia Triantafillos shaping pottery, or Sharon Walls explaining sewing, or Martin Saniga discussing his body painting and decoration, or Kris Dillard fashioning jewelry, or Carol Wiers in the cooking area or making stone tools, whoever is doing whatever in the village, I happily lead my groups to them whenever I can and happily observe what happens. (At every site at both of our museums, the interpreters are the heart of what we do. **They** are the ones who make the history come alive, especially for rapt young listeners, as no MPA can. When I entrust my people to an interpreter, I **know** their experience will be enhanced not only with knowledge and understanding, but also with seamless and sometimes intensified enthusiasm.)

Carol, greeting a B group, usually asks: "Have you gotten used to him by now?" Good ice-breaker with a B group.

Carol began working here as an MPA, but always wanted to work in the village and leaped at the opportunity to do so. Why? "Because I *love* the Stone Age." And you can tell she really does. She's a natural, at home in this environment. Sam McGowan, who taught Carol how to make tools, told me that she has a native knack for it, a "feel" for crafting stone and bone and shell.

* * *

Try to imagine the great Wahunsonacock and his family in 1607 sitting down to a great meal including beefsteak and ham, chicken and lamb, scrambled cheese and eggs, salted corn on the cob drenched in butter, wheat biscuits oozing with honey, with apples and peaches on the side and a choice of milk or tea.

Can you imagine that?

I can't. Only one of the items on that menu was known to the Powhatans in 1607. Which one?

I assume you picked corn. You might have been tempted – even though I clearly told you there was only one – to guess honey as well. Actually, the first honeybees didn't arrive in America until 1622, at Jamestown, not an insignificant fact if you happen to like honey, plus apples, peaches and an amazing host of other fruits and vegetables and flowers dependent on them. Beginning at Jamestown, the bees transformed and enriched the landscape of America as they swarmed westward.

* * *

Ending a visit to the village, I usually stop a school group at the walkway leading toward the ships, to make one final point regarding the Powhatans and others:

Do not look down on these people because of their "primitive" ways and "unsophisticated" cultures. Somewhere in your distant genealogy are people who lived like this. Looking down on these native people is like looking down on your own family, and that's just not right. I say: Admire them, for enduring the struggles of their times and for trying to love their young people and pass along the hope of a better future.

THE SHIPS

I **love** the rivers of Virginia. I especially love the James (still called by some the Powhatan) River.

Seeing it for the first time, some young people (real inlanders or West Coasters) wonder if it is the Chesapeake Bay, or even the Atlantic. I set them straight.

Standing at the end of our pier on a good day, you might see a canoe, a kayak or two, motorboats, sailboats, maybe even an ocean-going freighter heading upriver toward Richmond or downriver toward the ocean. On a really good day, you might see one of our ships under sail, a riveting sight.

Almost within a stone's throw is the island of great fame, with vehicles crossing the isthmus connecting the island to the mainland.

During Bacon's Rebellion, when the loyalist army moved to attack the island, Bacon's men tied the wives of loyalist officers to a barricade across the isthmus, delaying the attack, enabling the rebels to abandon the island.

During the Revolutionary War, British and French alternately unloaded men and supplies at Jamestown.

During the Civil War, the strategically placed island was held and fortified initially by the Confederates, who there secretly tested the metal plates being attached to the CSS Virginia (formerly the USS Merrimack); then by Union forces. Grant near Petersburg communicated with Lincoln at the War Department in Washington by telegraph via Jamestown. When Lincoln traveled to and from Grant's headquarters, I like to think he saw the old church tower on the island; I have no doubt that he fully understood the significance of the place, probably better than most people do today.

* * *

On December 20, 1606, three merchant ships crewed by 39 men and crammed with 105 passengers and other necessary cargo set sail from London down the Thames River toward the English Channel.

Their destination was somewhere in the vast Chesapeake Bay region in what the English called Virginia, in honor of Queen Elizabeth, during whose reign the men and women who were supposed to be landed in the Chesapeake were left instead on Roanoke Island, which is another story.

Six weeks after setting sail, buffeted by storms and contrary winds, the ships (with sails furled) were still in the English Channel, crew and passengers alike constantly seasick, virtually within sight of the homes of some of the men. There was understandable grumbling among the passengers, some of whom were ready to turn around.

One of the grumblers (for whatever reason), a former army captain, was such a trouble-maker that he was placed in confinement; during an island stop in the Caribbean, he was almost hanged; at Jamestown, he was released from confinement only when the formal orders of the Virginia Company were unsealed to reveal that the prisoner was one of the seven leaders of the colony.

I refer, of course, to John Smith, who at the age of 26 had already lived a life of such risk, danger and exotic adventure that modern "action heroes" pale in comparison. (A truthful telling of the story of Smith's life – before, during *and* after his Jamestown experience – will someday make a truly great movie.)

The voyage of about 6,000 miles, following the winds and currents of the Atlantic, required 144 days, much longer than expected.

Down below on the ships, the cramped, bored passengers lived and slept on crude mattresses atop other cargo, with few opportunities to visit the top deck and stretch their legs. The smell of seasickness and chamber pots and unwashed clothes and unbathed humanity was intense, but at least everybody stunk the same. Only one passenger died along the way, felled apparently by a heat stroke during a Caribbean island stopover.

After several weeks of exploring up and down the Powhatan River, making first contact with several tribes, the English settled on a 2,000-acre island about 50 miles from the ocean.

They chose that place in particular because (1) the river's deep main channel ran right up against the island, making anchorage simple and easing the task of loading and unloading cargo; (2) being inland meant a better chance of early warning if and when the Spanish came; and (3) nobody was living on the island.

There's a reason nobody was home. The natives had decided hundreds of years earlier that the island was not a good place to live, abandoning it and its swamps and its fevers and its unhealthy (because salty) groundwater.

In time, Wahunsonacock offered the English a better place to live, but the English declined the offer.

* * *

The three ships were the Nina, the Pinta and by this point someone or several people or the whole group interrupts me to protest that I'm wrong, though you might be surprised at how many younger and even a few older people either accept the information on faith or actually think I'm right.

For the record, the three ships were **not** the Nina, the Pinta, the Santa Maria, the Mayflower or the Minnow. They were: *Susan Constant*, the largest of the three, the flagship with about 17 crewmen and

54 passengers, captained by Christopher Newport, England's ablest mariner; *Godspeed,* the middle-sized ship with about 13 crewmen and 39 passengers, captained by Bartholomew Gosnold; and *Discovery*, the smallest with about nine crewmen and 12 passengers, captained by John Ratcliffe.

Only the Discovery remained behind, to be used in exploring the region, the others returning to England (and disappearing into the mist of history).

Diane Smith
The Susan Constant patiently awaits my group

Which ship was fastest? Think. Clue: The answer depends partly on keel design, but mostly on the number and surface area of the sails, which catch the wind, which makes the ship move. So the answer is . . . the Susan.

Tied to the pier inside our little cove are reproductions of the Susan, the Godspeed and the Discovery.

Across the cove is a fourth, well loved ship, Elizabeth; formerly Godspeed, she was actually sailed from London to Jamestown in 1985.

Our ships are to many of our visitors the stars of our show. It's easy to understand why. Merely building them was an obvious achievement. Interpreting them is a pleasant challenge. Maintaining them – and occasionally sailing one of them to near and distant places – requires a large, skilled and dedicated team, now ably captained by Eric Speth.

THE FORT

It goes without saying that the fort at our museum is not the 1607 fort found on the island. But it's worth noting that it isn't even the same fort I found on this location in 1999.

There's a new church in a different place, a new storehouse in a different place, a new well in a different place. A few years ago, soon after we finished building a fine small structure next to an older one, we tore both of them down and started building the fine big structure next to the exit gate.

Why all these changes? Simple: They make our fort conform more closely to what the archaeologists are discovering on the island.

Ours is meant to represent the fort as of 1610-14, following the Starving Time.

* * *

Entering the fort, I usually make a beeline for the blacksmith shop. I like the forge and the work done there, and I like the people who do it. I am particularly fond of watching and listening to Vince Petty, not only as he works the metal, but also as he engages the visitors. (Vince was in my MPA training class, but soon thereafter became a fort interpreter and is now our main blacksmith, and a very good one, or so it seems to me, but then how much do I know about blacksmithing except what Vince has taught me?)

If when I go to the forge an interpreter isn't there or is there but preoccupied, I know how to do the teaching myself. Now, I like to give credit where credit is due, and here I must say that almost everything I know about smithing I learned from Vince Petty, who knows next to nothing about it – No, seriously, folks, the information I am preparing to share and the manner of its sharing are based on Vince's excellent teaching. I've embellished it a bit, but it's still Vince's model.

I start by explaining to a group that the word "smith" comes from the old English verb "to smite"

– to hit, as a hammer hits metal. Thus, a person working in gold is a goldsmith. A person working in silver is a silversmith. A person working in copper is a . . . "Coppersmith." Yes. Tin? "Tinsmith."

Rubber? "Rubbersmith." Silly people! The English didn't have rubber; and besides, can you imagine a rubbersmith at work? Boing! Boing! Boing!

So what did the blacksmith do? "Made things . . . swords, nails, tools."

The blacksmith made **nothing**. Nails were made by nailers or nailsmiths, hammers by hammersmiths, chains by chainsmiths, locks by: "Locksmiths." Guns by: "Gunsmiths." Swords by: "Swordsmiths." Cutlers made knives and scissors. Armorers made armor. Farriers made horseshoes. Everything was made by a specialist who made only that thing, and the English settlers brought with them all of the necessary things made by the various smiths. (There were a lot of smiths back then, explaining why, when the English began using "normal" last names, a lot of Smiths emerged. It's the most common last name in the United States and the United Kingdom. The third most common name in Russia is Kuznetsov. What do you suppose it means? Duh.)

So why did the English bring two blacksmiths. What, exactly, did the blacksmith do? If you haven't figured it out by now, here's a clue: When you want a new car, you don't go to your mechanic and say build me a new car; but if you want that car repaired . . . "He fixes things!"

Now that we have that fact firmly established, it is true that we do make things at our forge. Our smiths are versatile repairmen, yes. But when we needed 5,000 or so 17th century nails for our newest building and couldn't find a 17th century hardware store open and didn't see anything similar at Ace or Lowe's or Home Depot, guess who made the nails? (Vince notes that while he might make about 200 nails in a good workday, with numerous distractions, a 17th century nailsmith might make 2,000 in a good but admittedly much longer and more grueling workday in much poorer conditions at far less pay with little or no hope of advancement.)

Given a choice between gray or orange or yellow or white, what is the most dangerous color of metal? Think. You've probably learned by now not to touch metal when it's white (actually burning at that color) or yellow or orange. But be advised that even when the color returns to normal gray the metal could still be 700 degrees. (Vince is asked if he ever gets burned. Sure, he says. One day, he pointed at several recent small burns he had gotten while working metal, then pointed at another and said it was his worst – from taking a pizza out of the oven the evening before!)

* * *

Among the 104 settlers were four carpenters, to build things which couldn't be brought over on the ships – like buildings and the fort itself – as well as to repair things which could be brought over. Carpenters were very important.

There were different types of carpenters, makers (wrights) of different things, like boatwrights and shipwrights and cartwrights and wain(wagon)wrights, not to mention coopers (barrel-makers) and other specialties. As with smithing, there's a lot more to the craft of carpentry than hammers and nails and saws. A carpenter's tool chest is large – and as splendid interpreter Dave Hanna likes to tell people: "But my most important tool is up here." He points to his head. "My experience, my knowledge, my ability."

Virginia must have seemed an especially spectacular wonderland to those carpenters. In stark contrast to England, where deforestation to provide fuel and ever more grazing land for sheep had removed 98 percent of the trees, 98 percent of Virginia was thick with trees, of all sorts, to provide a steady flow of wood and wood products to England, starting with the first return voyage. (It is rarely even a footnote in modern textbooks that in the 17th and 18th centuries Virginia acquired an international reputation for its natural beauty and resources, one of those threads of heritage which help to explain the special deep-seated sense of pride a Virginian sometimes reveals, even today.)

* * *

At least a brief walk through the guardhouse, with its display of weaponry and armor, is always a good idea during a tour; if there's time for an interpreter and one is available, it's a gem of a learning experience.

Cindy Ribeiro

The perfect photo of a musket firing

The 16-foot-long pike – the primary infantry weapon on the battlefields of Europe – proved useless in heavily forested Virginia against an enemy who wouldn't stand still. Thus, the primary

English weapon in Virginia proved to be the matchlock musket, with swords, knives and handguns available for close fighting with the Powhatans – and 24 cannon ready for the Spanish, to be awaited daily for many years.

The matchlock musket derives its name from the slow-burning rope, the match, which ignites the gunpowder. The close proximity of rope and powder can cause really bad accidents, such as happened to John Smith. An ember fell into his gunpowder bag. The explosion wounded him so severely he had to return to England, without saying goodbye to Pocahontas.

The effective range of the musket was about 100 yards, meaning a trained musketeer – and all of the men at early Jamestown were expected and if necessary trained to know how to use it – should hit a man-sized target at that distance. Didn't matter much where you hit him; the bullet would surely remove him from the action. A trained musketeer could fire three shots in a minute.

For close fighting, the Powhatans employed the blunt wooden tomahawk. At a distance, they fought with bow and arrow. They began in early childhood learning how to use these weapons. How good were they? With an effective range of about 40 yards, the Powhatan arrow, according to the English, *never* missed its target. But it might just glance off an Englishman's armor; and even if it hit an exposed area, it might not kill or even significantly disable him. An experienced archer could release 12 arrows in a minute.

Until the Powhatans acquired and learned how to use firearms – and they began trying to obtain them as soon as the English arrived – the military advantage, if slight, would belong to the English. (Virginia Indians had already experienced the deadly power of guns, demonstrated during earlier Spanish and English visits to the Chesapeake.)

One of the best weapons in England's arsenal – the famed English longbow – never became available in Virginia. A shipment of 600 got as far as Bermuda, but remained there, to prevent the Powhatans from learning the technology. (Similarly, the best American machinegun in World War I never reached the front lines, lest the technology fall into the hands of the Germans. On the flip side of the coin, Custer and his men were not only greatly outnumbered at the Little Big Horn, but also greatly outgunned. The Americans had revolvers and single-shot carbines. The Sioux had more than 40 different types of firearms, including Winchester repeating rifles, which the U.S. War Department considered too expensive to issue to its men. Not particularly relevant to Jamestown, but interesting. The ironies of history are part of what makes it so fascinating at times.)

The musket-firing is a routine feature in the fort. On the pier, a ship's rail gun is fired once or twice a day, or thrice as one of our ships returns home.

* * *

The storehouse helps to explain the establishment of an English presence in the region of the Chesapeake, initially financed by the Virginia Company. The main motivation was commercial, not just for personal or corporate gain but to improve England's position in Europe, where the dominating power of Spain and Portugal derived from the exploited riches of the so-called New World, particularly the gold and silver.

The very first day at Jamestown, the men began looking for gold and silver. Then and thereafter, they searched in vain, finding not a speck of either ore (unless you count fool's gold and you shouldn't). Ships returning to England during the early years carried wood and wood products, exotic furs, valuable sassafras roots for medicine and tea, and other ores, including low-quality but useful bog iron. Still, the Virginia Company was losing money, and men, with unpromising prospects.

The future of the English colony in Virginia, as in all of the other eventual mid-Atlantic colonies, was assured when Thomas Rolfe cultivated and sent to England the first tobacco grown in rich Virginia soil from seeds of a mild tobacco somehow obtained from the Spanish Caribbean. Tobacco hangs from the rafters of the storehouse. (Often, as in the barn at Yorktown, there is some initial wonderment when younger kids first see it, a wonderment I dispel.)

Until the inadequate management (and potential profit) of the scattered settlements along the James River obliged King James to make Virginia a royal colony, the Virginia Company gave the orders and provided the supplies, which explains the "VC" branded with numbers onto the barrels.

What's in the barrels? Clue: There is no wrong answer. So the answer is: Everything, from a wide variety of seeds to dried and pickled foods and salted meats, tools, weapons, gunpowder, clothing, you name it – even beverages, usually the first guess.

Why barrels instead of boxes? Think! . . . Clue: The smallest person in one of my groups can roll the biggest barrel at this museum. Got it?

Regarding the stuff hanging curiously from the rafters, I identify it as the basis of the success of the Virginia colony, but ask school groups: Is it good for you or bad for you? They know the answer. Then I ask: How long have we known this? They (including the adults) are usually surprised to learn that in 1604 King James wrote in "A Counterblaste to Tobacco" not only that it's foul-smelling, which it is, but also (based on autopsy results) that it's bad for your health, particularly your brain and lungs.

* * *

I like to end a tour of the Settlement in the church. It seems appropriate.

Religion was more than ordinarily important to the people during the early years at Jamestown. In uncertain times in a dangerous place, one tends to pray a lot; and the situation in Virginia was *very* uncertain and dangerous.

Initially, church attendance was expected. During the period of martial law, attendance was required, with punishments for nonattendance without a good excuse – for a first absence, loss of food for a day; for a second offense, a whipping (and they knew how to give whippings in those days); for a third, involuntary servitude at hard labor for several months, or death, though there is no record of anyone being executed for such a crime.

As the wooden crest over the chancel indicates, being at Jamestown in the early years required loyalty to King James not only as head of state but also as head of the Church of England. Hence, Catholics (particularly Spanish ones) were not welcome here. We tend to forget nowadays that in those times the Catholics and Protestants were fighting and killing one another, not unlike the Sunni and the Shi'a within Islam today. Tolerance among the Christians in Virginia would come later in the 17th century (after the Catholics had already established Maryland).

That first summer at Jamestown, blacksmith James Read in the only recorded instance of his using his hammer hit the governor with it, and was condemned to die like a yeoman, by hanging. In the first plea bargain in Virginia history, Read avoided the noose by outing as a Spanish spy (on the basis of evidence not entered in the record) Captain George Kendall, a member of the governing council. Being a gentleman, Kendall was shot; rank even then had its privileges. (Was he really a spy? Yes, according to a section of Spanish archives translated in recent years; in fact, there were two, the other being an unnamed Irishman. If anything, this helps to prove that the English venture in Virginia did not happen in a vacuum or by chance.)

* * *

It was probably in the first church at Jamestown, which ours is meant to represent, that John and Rebecca (formerly Pocahontas) Rolfe were married in 1614. Only a few years ago, the archaeologists on the island announced that they had found the first church; a couple of years ago, they announced that they had found its chancel, and thus the exact spot on which the Rolfes were wed; this past year, on the 400th anniversary of the wedding, it was re-enacted, on the exact spot, in a ceremony featuring a young woman of the Pamunkey people.

* * *

With adult groups and with students old enough to understand what I'm talking about, I customarily end a tour (as usually promised at the beginning of a tour) by providing a glimpse into the future; with a school group, I also customarily ask the teacher's permission to do so.

What follows is not exactly that glimpse, which on a tour must be much briefer and less detailed. But this isn't a tour, is it? It's a book, and we've got more time to take a closer look at the situation.

A Glimpse into the Future

"Democracy"

The concept of democracy, in whatever form, has surfaced at various times and places in history. The Athenian model established the common-sense premise on which any democracy must be based if it hopes to endure – that the citizens making the decisions must be well informed and educated in detail to make good, wise decisions, in war and peace. (To some students of history and civics, the Greek concept of democracy is linked closely to the Roman republican virtues of public service.)

In the early 17th century, there were no true democracies in the world, and limited democracies in only a handful of places, and the world was constantly at war over one thing or another or nothing at all, driven mostly by vanity, greed and religious differences.

In the latter 18th century, the emergence of the United States of America, with its resonating Declaration of Independence and Constitution and Bill of Rights, created a radical new model of democracy, or at least the idealistic, optimistic outlines thereof. The success of the American experiment was by no means certain. External pressures and internal tensions, particularly over slavery, menaced the republic from the beginning.

In the 19th century, the compassion and genius of Abraham Lincoln not merely liberated the slaves, but more importantly kept the Union intact in a world still ruled by autocrats and still unfriendly to the idea of human rights and democratic governance, a world constantly at war.

When the Great World War erupted, there were only 10 democracies in the world, nations ruled essentially by their people. It became known as the war to save democracy, which it did, though it certainly did not stop wars and threats of wars between nations.

Hence: World War II, the triumph of the peculiar alliance of democracy and capitalism **and** autocracy and communism over Nazism and fascism and imperialism – and then, the onset of the Cold War, the global confrontation between the nuclear superpowers the United States and the Soviet Union and their allies and client or subject nations. The symbol of this confrontation was the Berlin Wall.

I ask the adults in my groups if they expected the Berlin Wall to come down or the Soviet Union to collapse in their lifetimes, and I ask them to answer loudly if it's a school group, so the kids can hear them. The answer is almost unanimously no, of course; the rare few who say yes usually acknowledge it was mostly a vague if strong hope.

I predicted it. Studying history helps you to know what to look for, so you can see it coming. I saw it coming.

The Recent Past

In 1974, I did perceive a fundamental shift in the course of human events and began sharing with anyone who cared to listen my view that the Berlin Wall would come down and the Soviet Union would collapse, with little or no bloodshed, within 15-20 years.

As the years passed and what I considered to be solid supportive evidence accumulated, I expanded my view with increasing detail and confidence. I do not recall anyone believing me; the idea was just too outrageous, almost laughably so. My brother-in-law Jay Aldhizer, who at the height of the Cold War served for eight years in liaison between the FBI and CIA, didn't believe me. Neither did my brother-in-law Lieb Lotterhos, a Strategic Air Command B-52 pilot whose intended ground zero was Red

Square in Moscow. I was not offended by their disbelief. I could not blame them.

The Berlin Wall was torn down in 1989. The Soviet Union finally collapsed in 1991. Since then, within the former Soviet sphere of influence as elsewhere, the concept of democracy has dramatically if sometimes awkwardly advanced. Our own democracy isn't perfect, and one size doesn't fit all. Wherever it is attempted, it must be a work in progress, sometimes requiring patience by the people, sometimes demanding impatience.

Footnote 1: When in 1991 the news came that the hard-liners had staged a coup against Gorbachev's reformers and Yeltsin's democrats, I happened to be with a CIA friend. He was certain the hard-liners were truly back in power, that the reformers and democrats would now be crushed. I advised him not to worry, that the coup would collapse within 48-72 hours. He didn't believe me. It collapsed in 60.

Footnote 2: Retired from the FBI, Jay with his wife Peggy accompanied one of my Visitor Services tours at the Settlement. In the church, in front of the group, he good-naturedly apologized for not believing me earlier. Such a fine man, and friend.

Special Footnote: Retired from the Air Force, Lieb had occasion to visit Moscow in the early 1990s, recognizing the landmarks he had been trained to spot on the low-level bombing run which would have eradicated metropolitan Moscow.

One evening, he and an American associate had an enjoyable dinner with an official of the Russian Foreign Ministry, a very amiable fellow (who according to Lieb "spoke better English than you or me – without a trace of an accent"). The official was understanding of Lieb's Cold War mission, and noted that he knew what it was like to *live* at ground zero. He invited the two Americans to be his guests the next day on a special occasion.

Thus, on the 4th of July, with a Russian symphony orchestra performing an outdoor concert of American patriotic music, Lieb stood in Red Square. He cried. Recently, I learned by asking him for the first time how he felt at that moment. "I never expected to be there **at ground zero**," he softly replied, still obviously affected by that moment. "It was very touching." (He is, as almost every veteran I've ever met is, a good man of peace and reason.)

And only recently did Lieb have occasion to mention for the first time the Russian official's vital role in his being in Red Square on that special occasion, and his name. The gentleman is Sergei Lavrov, current Foreign Minister of the Russian Federation. Thank you, Sergei, for your kindness to my friend.

The Immediate Present

As recently as the early 1980s, there were still only 45 democracies.

Today, there are some 120 democracies in the world and a whole lot less war and threat of war between nations than there used to be. This is not coincidental. The explanation is simple: Democracies do not go to war against each other. With the very arguable exception of the American Civil War, it has never happened.

The nations of Europe wrote the book on war. But if you ask any European if there will ever be another war among the people there, the answer is almost always no. There is some lingering concern about the Balkans, but otherwise it seems that the people of Europe have effectively abolished war among themselves – which once upon a time was virtually unthinkable – and are quite happy about it! This profoundly powerful fact is insufficiently understood and appreciated. It should help to give us greater hope for the future everywhere.

I decline at this time to comment in detail on the situation among the peoples of Islam. The new movement toward democracy is encouraging; the deep-rooted animosity and violence between Sunni and Shi'a is not. Rational resolution of the problems within Islam – and I do prefer to think it is possible – will be a major factor in determining where humanity as a whole goes from here.

I must say this: Mohammed and Jesus would weep at the violence done in their names!!!

The Possible Future

If all goes well (or well enough), the future of humanity is actually quite bright, or should be.

Quite aside from what we are capable of accomplishing here on Earth, we are just about ready for another attempt at the real breakout into space.

For the moment, forget about the Space Shuttle and the International Space Station, and don't be distracted by the near-term prospect of expensive but brief tourism ventures. Think bigger – much, much bigger – and bring the welfare of the whole of humanity into your thinking.

Forty years ago, outside of NASA and well beyond NASA's range of planning, a few people began exploring the idea of building very large structures in space, using the abundant raw materials of space to do it.

The idea became the High Frontier concept pioneered by physicist Gerard O'Neill of Princeton, engaging many bright minds in many academic disciplines in some major-league thinking – huge farms in space to grow food more cheaply than on Earth, to end hunger; huge solar power satellites to provide cheap electricity, to end our dependence on fossil and nuclear fuels; permanent human communities with Earth-like interior conditions and gravity, the first one designed to accommodate 10,000 people.

Perhaps a bit fancifully but nonetheless a bit plausibly, I say to my school groups that if all goes well (or well enough) they might be able to go with their grandchildren or great-grandchildren someday on a great vacation in space, from the shores of New Hawaii to the ski slopes of New England to a really historic tourist attraction – that first permanent community.

Question: What would some people like to name it?

While you search your fine mind for the answer, I note that for several years I was associated with Gerry O'Neill and his extraordinary team of practical-minded visionaries. One evening, Gerry and I discussed various possible names for the first community and the reasons for considering them. At the end of this exercise, I asked him: "Gerry, what would you name it?" He thought for a moment, then looked me in the eye and said: "Bill, I would name it New Jamestown." (Gerry had a strong bias toward democracy and free enterprise, and the sharing of knowledge. At a time when the chancellor of Austria was urging other European leaders to read Gerry's book **The High Frontier**, Gerry was invited to address the Soviet Academy of Science, at his convenience; he flatly refused the invitation, in opposition to communism.)

I seldom recalled that conversation until I became an MPA. It seemed natural, indeed mandatory, to find a place within my teaching routine for Gerry's wishful thinking.

Footnote: One of Gerry's associates, economist Peter Vajk, wrote a book entitled **Doomsday Has Been Canceled**. Not enough people have read it.

NASA

A community in space

POCAHONTAS

I refer not to the ferryboat but to Amonute (her birth name), also known as Matoaka (her spiritual name meaning Flower between the Rivers), also known as Pocahontas (her nickname meaning

Playful One), also known as Rebecca Rolfe, daughter of the great Wahunsonacock.

Very soon after I became an MPA, I asked some students (and adults) if there happened to be a descendant of Pocahontas among us. And it happened there was, a girl who knew her family genealogy; she was, as I recall, a Bolling.

I began asking the question of most of my American groups above the fourth grade. To this date (excluding want-to-be descendants and folks uncertain of their genealogy), 182 students and adults have credibly identified themselves as grandchildren of Pocahontas, including one descended from Pocahontas and Kokoum (from whom the entertainer Wayne Newton is also descended). One group included not only a descendant of Pocahontas and Rolfe, but also a descendant of the minister, the Reverend Alexander Whitaker, who married them; neither visitor previously knew about the other's genealogy.

One busy day on the pier, a woman pointed out to me a group of 17 descendants on the Susan, enjoying a family reunion. I don't include them in my count.

I do include Elizabeth Bolling Skelley of Texas, whom I met at the portrait of Pocahontas on the day President Bush was here in 2007 to deliver what proved to be a fine speech, especially in its strong advocacy of democracy, perfect for that truly great occasion. Elizabeth, a brilliant woman (about whom

I later learned more by Googling her), was planning to visit some of her Powhatan kin while in the area. So guess who wrote the core of the President's great speech on that truly great occasion? A descendant of the woman who made this all possible wrote it, that's who. Of course!

Speaking of 2007 . . .

2007!

You might've heard about it.

It was in the newspapers and on radio and television and the Internet.

It was on the cover of the Smithsonian magazine, National Geographic, Time and U.S. News & World Report, among others.

It commanded the presence of the Queen of England, and the President of the United States of America, and assorted other dignitaries and common folk.

It required hundreds of uniformed local and state police – and who knows how many more security personnel (including Secret Service and Scotland Yard) blending in with the common folk.

It lasted for most of the year but focused on the 13th of May, the 400th anniversary of the English setting foot permanently on the nearby island.

Most of "it" is a pleasant blur. I had 288 tours that year, 253 of them at the Settlement, many of the latter being 90-minute Visitor Services tours of the outdoor sites.

A few memories do come to mind distinctly enough to suggest they're worth sharing.

* * *

At the shelter on the pier at the end of yet another Visitor Services tour, I was speaking to a typically very large crowd when I noticed a smiling face which seemed very familiar. I paused.

"You, sir, wearing the cap. You look a lot like my state senator."

He took off his cap.

"You *are* my state senator!"

I walked over to him, shared a hug with him (of course), then announced: "Ladies and gentlemen, permit me to introduce my friend Tommy Norment, member of the Virginia Senate and president of Jamestown 2007. This is one of the people most responsible for all this. Let's hear it for him!"

The applause was enthusiastic. Tommy seemed pleased.

As the crowd dispersed, an out-of-state visitor remarked: "That's impressive. I never see my state senator . . . I'm not even sure of his name."

* * *

The next day, the 13th of May, President Bush delivered his fine speech during a program which included a 400-piece orchestra and a 1,607-voice choir.

I noted that among the local, state and national dignitaries sharing the platform were four people who within the previous year had spoken to the Friday Luncheon Group I have coordinated for many years, and a fifth – Tommy Norment – who would speak to us later that month.

I also noted that the only dignitary the President hugged, and only half-hugged at that, was Tommy, whom I had hugged much better the day before!

* * *

Not long after becoming an MPA, I was obliged to wait at Kinko's for my printing job to be processed. I walked over to a nearby table and asked the woman sitting there if I might join her. Smiling softly, she motioned me to do so, so I did.

And that's how I met Shirley "Little Dove" Custalow McGowan.

I had heard of her, but knew very little about her. A Pamunkey, an advocate for the Powhatan people, some sort of spiritual leader. Oh, yes, and a member of the board of directors of the Jamestown-Yorktown Foundation.

We chatted for about two hours, well beyond when our jobs were done. I knew I was in the presence of someone very special. We finally parted, saying we hoped our paths would cross again. I went home and told my wife: "I have fallen in love!" I told Shirley's son Sam, too, the next time I encountered him. I thought it was the decent thing to do. (Reader: You would love her, too.)

Subsequently, at the statue of Opechancanough, I began referencing Shirley on some of my tours, telling my groups about the time I met her, how I was awed by her wisdom and compassion, so much that I considered her one of the most exceptional human beings I have ever known. It was hard to put into words.

Our paths crossed again in 2007, under the huge tent serving as a temporary staff cafeteria, a very busy, very noisy scene. Across that crowded room, our eyes met, and we smiled, and began making our way toward each other, until finally we met at the center, hugged, and exchanged greetings and good wishes . . . I confess: I was almost in tears. I don't know why. I do know that *she remembered me!* I felt honored.

One day, in the gallery with a group of middle school Muslim boys from the Islamic Saudi Academy in northern Virginia, I began to tell the group about Shirley "**Little Dove Custalow!**" a boy loudly interrupted me to say. "I **know** her! I've **met** her! She's the **greatest** person I've ever met!!" . . . I rest my case.

* * *

A friend arriving one morning presented a huge bag of Hershey's chocolate kisses to some stern state troopers manning one of the entrance stations. When I arrived a couple of hours later, the boys were happily gobbling down the last kisses in that really huge bag.

* * *

The number of people on my Visitor Services tours tended to increase significantly as I went along. It was not uncommon to begin with 35-40 and finish with 70-75, or more. Other guides reported similar experiences.

One day, as I led my people out of the fort toward the ships, an interpreter with a serious expression on her face asked a question MPAs often jokingly hear: "Are you aware you're being followed? I'm serious. Look behind you." I did . . . Many more than a hundred people were following me.

* * *

One week, there were 600 antique automobiles in town − and 3,000 Harley-Davidsons. The antiques were not a problem. But the Harleys loved riding on the ferryboats, and it sounded like all of them were crossing the river repeatedly, and the constant roar of them sometimes drowned out all attempts to teach effectively in the village. All week!

* * *

At the end of two of my Visitor Services tours, someone or several in the group said I should run for President, and others quickly agreed, and all of them promised to vote for me. I declined to run. One of the best decisions I've ever made.

* * *

In the crowded church, I finished my Visitor Services tour with some optimistic comments about democracy and the future, including the potential human benefits of space development, and routinely asked if there were any final questions.

A gentleman stepped into the aisle and, posturing as he spoke in a refined English accent, asked (as on the floor of the House of Commons while grilling the Prime Minister) a question so complex in its syntax and so convoluted in its reasoning that even though I suspected what he meant I really could not understand it and told him so, as did several others in the audience.

With a hint of impatience, he rephrased the question in a manner which made his meaning clear, confirming my suspicion. Basically, he challenged my optimism – particularly regarding the development of space, which he said would only enrich the capitalists and exploit the people. With confidence, he awaited my answer.

Everyone in the church awaited my answer.

(Now, it is true that about 40 years ago I mostly shelved the methodology of debate in favor of the methodology of discussion in problem-solving and decision-making. Prior to then, however, I had considerable experience and some success in competitive debate. I also happened to be very familiar with parliamentary-style debating, and had in fact been a member of the College of William and Mary team hosting, and in my opinion besting, a team from Oxford University. So how should I respond?)

I said that he and I had different opinions based on different views of the world and of the people – and a very different basis of knowledge on which to be making sweeping judgements.

He restated his arguments, unwilling to give ground. I restated mine, wondering how this might end. (It had become quite clear to me and probably to almost everyone else there that he knew little if anything about advanced space research and development, whereas at least I seemed to know *something*.)

Finally, he threw the question at me: "But it is really only your opinion, isn't it?"

"Yes, it is," I readily conceded, since he was right. Then, noticing him sense victory, I added: "But it is an *educated* opinion."

And that seemed to give me – and my view of the future – the edge, to the unspoken but visible relief of the congregation, whom I simply could not disappoint.

The debate, such as it was, ended.

Smithsonian American Art Museum,
Gift of Olin Dows

In this early 19th century scene by artist John Chapman, an ox-cart moves along the road from Williamsburg into Yorktown in the distance. To the right of the cart is the future site of the Yorktown Victory Center.

We are in the very midst of a revolution,
the most complete, unexpected and remarkable
of any in the history of nations.
John Adams

Chapter 3: Yorktown Victory Center

The Place

In 1976, to help the nation celebrate the 200th anniversary of the formal beginning of the American Revolution and the independence of the United States, the Commonwealth of Virginia opened the Yorktown Victory Center on 22 acres donated by Nick and Mary Matthews, Greek-born American patriots who are now buried on the property. (Their internationally famous restaurant, Nick's Seafood Pavilion, was a casualty of Hurricane Isabel.)

Currently, again putting our money where our mouth is, the Commonwealth of Virginia is investing more than $41 million in a total transformation of the museum, comparable to what happened at Jamestown Settlement. The new facility overlooking the lovely York River (the Pamunkey River to the Powhatans) will become known in 2016 as the American Revolution Museum at Yorktown.

It looks good on paper. I suspect the reality will be magnificent. (One reason for my confidence in the ultimate product is my appreciation of the *process* of planning it. As at Jamestown, the transformation at Yorktown will reflect a widespread effort to solicit suggestions, ideas, notions, proposals and such from the rank-and-file employees who deal with the visitors on a daily basis. This sort of employee empowerment and participation is commendable, and productive.

Adjacent to Colonial National Historical Park, the Victory Center originally included a ticket-purchasing building with gift shop and a larger structure with an indoor gallery and administrative offices, plus the outdoor sites – a timeline and the military encampment.

Subsequently, a small farm was added. When I read about this in the newspaper, I wondered why the people running that place were adding a farm to a museum devoted to a military action. Now, I think it's one of the smartest decisions we've ever made. I'll tell you why when we go there.

At the beginning of a tour here, I ask my groups if we are on the battlefield. They almost always say no. I say yes – that the mound of earth across the road was in 1781 a British redoubt, manned by Royal Welsh Fusiliers controlling the main road into Yorktown from the west; that twice, soldiers of the French Royal Deux Ponts Regiment attacked that position and were repulsed; that indeed, on the ground on which we stand men fought and bled and died so we could be here. I trust that the new museum will do a better job of letting visitors know the historical significance of the site itself.

THE LOOP

As at Jamestown, the action at Yorktown begins on the loop, wherever it may happen to be. The old parking area is now a construction site, so the loop is in a new parking area. Eventually, it will be elsewhere.

THE FARM

I like to begin a tour on the farm. Why? Because that's where almost everybody in British America lived, on a farm.

At this point in time, there were approximately three million people in British America, 600,000 of them in Virginia, making Virginia by far the largest, wealthiest and most influential of the colonies. The biggest city in Virginia was Williamsburg, with fewer than 2,000 residents. If you want to understand how people then lived, thought, felt, made decisions, it begins with the farm.

Ours reflects the lifestyle of a middlin' farmer, not poor, not rich but moving upward.

A farm is by definition a place where you grow stuff – most importantly, food for your family; then, food for your critters; then, if have enough acreage and labor, a "cash crop" – in this region, probably tobacco.

The nearest neighbor might be a mile away, with only occasional opportunities for neighbors and extended families to get together. If you are a child at this time, you are part of the labor force, likely never to learn how to read and write and reckon numbers. Of necessity, your best friend is probably your brother or sister (an unthinkable thought to many youngsters nowadays). Families were closer then. They had to be.

* * *

In the main house, the open windows provide the air-conditioning, and the fireplace provides central heating, but the fact remains: When the weather was hot, you were hot; and when it was cold, you were cold. As for the light switch, forget about it, and everything associated with it.

Some of the objects inside an 18th house were made on the farm, or elsewhere in the colony. Others were made in the Mother Country, and could be made only there.

Here was the basic "deal" back then, the economic arrangement between the British in America and the British back home: The Americans produced stuff from our vast natural resources – wood, ores, furs, tobacco, cotton – and in exchange the Mother Country provided the Americans with the better things of life – foods grown only elsewhere, including molasses, tea, coffee and chocolate; most of the books and better furniture and musical instruments; everything made of iron and steel, including the tools for farming; and guns, absolutely necessary for hunting game and dealing with the Indians; plus, of course, gunpowder.

The arrangement worked well enough for a long time, enabling Britain and the constantly growing colonies to prosper, the population in British America doubling every 20 years. And besides the economic benefits, it was **good** to be British. Who had the best navy and army in the world? We did. Who had a limited monarchy and a parliamentary system of government and trial by jury and all of the many other privileges of being a British citizen? We did. Who produced Shakespeare? We did. Yes, it was **good** to be British, and don't forget it.

* * *

Among other things, the decision to do battle with Britain meant the disruption of all trade and the collapse of the tobacco market, devastating the economy of the mid-Atlantic colonies until peace could be negotiated or alternative markets developed.

It also meant, in 1775, an end to the importation of gunpowder, creating an immediate crisis for the rebel cause: Nobody in America knew how to make the stuff. George Washington's so-called army outside Boston could not fight because of the shortage of gunpowder. One of Washington's generals wrote: "Powder! Ye gods, give us powder!" In Virginia, Patrick Henry appealed for a permanent Virginia militia – and for somebody to make gunpowder.

The first Virginian to make the attempt was a 75-year-old man named Benjamin Clement, whose home still stands (though in poor condition) in the little town of Hurt near Alta Vista. Clement and neighbor Charles Lynch perfected a formula and began making gunpowder, as Lynch confirmed in a letter to the editor of the Virginia Gazette in Williamsburg. Washington reportedly sent a note of thanks to Clement, who happens to be my great-great-great-great-great-great grandfather.

Did Benjamin Clement make a difference? Do you make a difference? You make a difference every day, in many ways. Someone once said that great opportunities for serving humanity come rarely, but little ones surround us daily. And as Margaret Meade said in a gem of insight well known but always worth repeating: "Never doubt that a small group of thoughtful, committed citizens can change the world. Indeed, it is the only thing that ever has."

* * *

The kitchen outbuilding (where an interpreter is always available to do a far better job than I could do) is separate from the main house not only to reduce the risk of fire, as commonly assumed, but also, more importantly, to remove from the house the heat, smoke and fumes of continuous cooking in the pre-microwave age.

It was also the pre-refrigerator age, which meant it was critical to know how to preserve a wide variety of foods – meats, vegetables, fruits – by salting or drying or pickling.

* * *

Inside the tobacco barn, you can see the cash crop hanging from the rafters and crammed into a hogshead barrel. I talk about the labor-intensive process of cultivating tobacco (beginning with a seed smaller than the period at the end of this sentence), its central role in the barter economy of the time, the great fleets of ships which assembled seasonally in the rivers of Virginia to transport the golden weed home in protective convoys.

As at Jamestown, I ask: Is this stuff good for you or bad for you? You probably know the answer by now.

THE TIMELINE

Alas, the old timeline – three sheltered areas with great visuals focusing on Treaty and Taxes and Tea – is gone, replaced by the new parking area. We still can and do address the three topics at stations along the pathway near the farm.

Treaty

In the mid-1750s, North America was divided between Spanish Mexico, French Canada and British America. Mind you, the Europeans *claimed* all of this vastness; they did not *possess* most of it; the Indians still occupied and controlled most of it, and considered it theirs.

Britain and France had been going to war against each other for hundreds and hundreds of years (one of their wars lasting more than a hundred years), and it was only a matter of time until they went to war again, to decide who would control the rich resources and possibilities of America.

In 1754, a 22-year-old Virginia militia colonel led a detachment of men into the disputed western territory, to discourage any French encroachment. The Virginians encountered a small party of French soldiers and Indian allies, and without asking the intruders any questions the young colonel gave his men the order to fire, firing the first shot himself, winning the brief fight. He should not have done it.

The French were on a diplomatic mission, protected by international law.

That spark ignited what became known in America as the French and Indian War, in Europe as the Seven Years War, the first real world war, fought by Britain and France and their allies around the globe. Britain, guided by the brilliant Prime Minister William Pitt and the able young King George III, won the war, ending with the Treaty of Paris in 1763 – and British America exulted. It was never better to be British, anywhere. The future of the Empire – more than half of it in America – was never brighter.

But there was a problem: Are wars free? No. Somebody had to pay for fighting that war, and for maintaining about 7,500 British regular soldiers in America to discourage any renewed French ambition as well as to help the colonists deal with the Indians.

* * *

With a school group, I sometimes take a $1 bill out of my wallet and offer it to anyone who can tell me the name of the young Virginia colonel who fired that first shot out in the wilderness that led to the Seven Years War that led to the American Revolution that led to the French Revolution that led to the Napoleonic Wars and the path of history we are traveling today.

Few people, young or old, know the answer. As I grasp the banknote with both hands and make the answer manifest, somebody eventually guesses correctly and gets the dollar; once, without waiting for the question, a whole class answered instantly, their teacher having been with me before, so I gave the dollar bill to the teacher and told her that determining how to divide it was her problem, not mine, since she had created it.

You *do* know the answer by now, don't you? Think. He's on our 25-cent coin, too.

Isn't it amazing that the greatest man of that great chapter in history started it?

Taxes

The recent war and the stationing of regular troops were of great benefit to British Americans, who paid only a small fraction of the taxes paid by the people in Britain, so many members of Parliament reasoned that the Americans should help foot the bill. Early in 1765, the parliamentary majority enacted the Stamp Act, to take effect on November 1; the minority, including Mr. Pitt, vigorously opposed the measure, saying it was constitutionally wrong and would cause trouble.

It was, and it did.

The law, already in effect in Britain, was simple: Every time an American bought a deck of playing cards, or a newspaper or pamphlet or book, or conducted legal business requiring official documents, a tax stamp had to be embossed on special paper. Simple. But as soon as news of the law reached America, the grumbling began. I ask my groups (whatever their composition): "Let me hear you grumble." Most grumble at least a little.

It wasn't so much the idea of being taxed as the way it was being done.

The original Jamestown Charter of 1607 contained a royal guarantee "that all persons living in the colonie shall have all the liberties and immunities the same as if they had been borne or lived in England," and Virginians especially never forgot it. The tradition of representative colonial legislatures deciding direct taxes was deeply imbedded; likewise, the tradition of throwing out the rascals who tax unwisely and electing new rascals. Thus, arguably in violation of not only colonial but also British principles, the Stamp Act represented . . . taxation without representation.

But that's not all. Any alleged breaker of the law would be tried not by a local judge in a local court in front of a jury of his neighbors, but in Canada by a military judge according to military law. But that's not all. The tax must be paid in *specie*, hard cash, coins − and there weren't a lot of coins in circulation in barter-based British America, and many of those coins weren't even British!

119

So again I ask my groups: "**Now** let me hear you grumble!" They lustily do.

But all of the grumbling in the world won't do you a bit of good. What the situation in 1765 required was a man smart enough and brave enough to stand up for America and tell the Parliament and the King what was wrong with the Stamp Act. Throughout the colonies, people looked to Virginia for leadership. In Virginia, they looked to Hanover County, to a young lawyer already well known for eloquently standing up to the authorities.

Problem: Patrick Henry was not a member of Virginia House of Burgesses, soon to meet in Williamsburg to discuss the Stamp Act. Solution: The burgess from Hanover County resigned so a special election could be held to elect Mr. Henry to the House of Burgesses just in time for him to get on his horse and ride hard to Williamsburg to arrive just in time for the beginning of the session.

On the 29th of May, his 29th birthday, Henry prepared seven resolutions strongly condemning the Stamp Act. On the 30th, he delivered a great speech, interrupted by accusations of treason from some of the men who would be leading the rebellion a few years later. Henry rode home the next day, having done what he came to do. (Jefferson, an eyewitness on the 30th, later observed: "The ball of revolution in Virginia was set in motion when Mr. Henry rose to speak.")

Soon, Henry's resolutions were being published in the newspapers of America and Britain, rallying the opposition on both sides of the Atlantic, which in America included intimidation of the men appointed to collect the taxes; the men quit. The law went into effect on November 1. Publishers ignored it. Courts closed, because people stopped getting married and doing other legal business. Resistance was widespread and emphatic. And in all of British America, how many sheets of paper embossed with the hated stamp were sold? I suspect you know the answer.

For the first time in history, a whole people had stood up and said what to their government? I know you know the answer.

"So are we ready for independence?" I ask my groups. Yes, they proclaim.

"No!" I say. "Almost nobody is thinking about independence – but we *will* have equal rights as British citizens! Remember: It's **good** to be British."

Back home, the reaction to American defiance was sharply divided. The parliamentary majority, forced to repeal the Stamp Act, was angry; the minority was elated. "I rejoice that America has resisted!" William Pitt declared. But the majority remained in power.

* * *

Incidentally, that great speech of 1765 was not, as some naturally guess, the "Give me liberty or give me death" speech of 1775.

One day with a group of fifth-graders from Richmond (where the latter speech was delivered at St. John's Church), I began to quote the ending of that famed oration: "Gentlemen may cry, Peace! Peace!" I began, shutting my mouth as the whole class continued: "But there is no peace! The war is actually begun! The next gale that sweeps from the north will bring to our ears the clash of resounding arms! Our brethren are already in the field! Why stand we here idle? What is it that gentlemen wish? What would they have? Is life so dear, or peace so sweet, as to be purchased at the price of chains and slavery? Forbid it, Almighty God! I know not what course others may take; but as for me, give me liberty or give me death!"

I was appropriately wowed!

Tea

In the years following the Stamp Act debacle, the majority in Parliament enacted a series of measures to collect revenues from the Americans *and* to show them who was boss; and the Americans contrived ways to resist, including the smuggling of untaxed goods into the colonies. Respected merchants, men like John Hancock of Boston, were respectable smugglers.

Which brings us to the Tea Party. "You know about the Tea Party, don't you?" I ask. Yes, some reply, in Boston. "Boston?!" I declare. "They had a tea party in Boston?! Teacher, is that correct? . . . Because I'm talking about the *Yorktown* Tea Party!"

That was the danger of what those merchants up in Boston did late in 1773 when, led by men usually described as "dressed up like Indians," they dumped those 242 casks of tea into the harbor. They set a bad example, inflaming the spirit of opposition elsewhere and leading eventually to tea parties at other colonial ports – Charleston, Annapolis (where the offending ship was torched) and Yorktown.

In 1774, even before those other tea parties had been held, Parliament closed the port of Boston (with 40,000 people the biggest city in British America), a crippling economic blow. Virginia led the protest, beginning in Williamsburg on June 10 with a special service at Bruton Parish Church attended by the House of Burgesses, the feeling being: Whatever the authorities can do to our brothers and sisters in Boston, they could do to us in Virginia.

Relief supplies, the staples of life, poured into Boston. Militia units began encamping and fortifying their positions outside the city, confronting the British regulars inside. Fighting would soon begin.

"So **now** are we ready for independence?" I ask. Yes! "No!" I say.

***

This is a good time to ask: George III – good king or bad king?

Bad king, many say, understandably influenced by the Declaration of Independence and other negative references. Good king, I think, an able good-hearted man trying to do his kingly duty as he understood it, influenced by the parliamentary majority which really set the policy. Charles the current Prince of Wales considers George III a role model, and Charles' new grandson is named for him.

***

This is also a good time to ask: Lord Charles Cornwallis – good guy or bad guy?

Bad guy, some say, probably knowing only that he was a loser at Yorktown. Good guy, I think.

When Parliament voted on the Stamp Act, who voted against it? Who voted against all of the majority's retaliatory acts? When war came and many army and navy officers resigned from service rather than fight in what they considered an unjust war, who remained loyal to his king and ably served in America during the early years of the war? Who, on a recess from the war, went home to be with his ailing wife, who died and left instructions that his name was not to be put on her headstone – because he was too pro-American?! Who was not blamed for the defeat at Yorktown (his only loss) and went on to serve Britain with great distinction, particularly as Viceroy of India, where today there are statues of him in three cities? I think you get the point . . . A very good guy, I do believe.

One day, an eighth-grade girl sitting in the Tea pavilion proudly identified herself as a descendant of Lord Cornwallis. A year later, an eighth-grade girl from another state, sitting in the same spot, likewise identified herself as a descendant of Lord Cornwallis – and of Elbridge Gerry, a Signer of the Declaration. Both girls obviously were well acquainted with his lordship; neither had heard about the tombstone.

Please Note Well

Nowadays, nobody seems to wonder or care why some of those respectable Bostonians "dressed up as Indians" to do their provocative deed. Everybody should know and care.

They didn't do it (as Wikipedia says) to "disguise" their identities, and they weren't just *any* Indians. They were well known citizens attired as *Mohawks* to make a deliberate political statement to the authorities.

In youth, I happened to learn about the Mohawk aspect of the Boston Tea Party in a footnote in a school textbook published in the mid-19th century, since when this significant detail has been reduced to less than a footnote. And I did not begin to appreciate its full significance until very recent years.

The trouble-makers in Boston demonstrated a spirit of independence best explained by Charles Mann in his remarkable book **1491**: "The framers of the Constitution, like most colonists in what would become the United States, were pervaded by Indian ideals and images of liberty," and recognized among the native people "a level of autonomy unknown in Europe."

Research Assignment – Do yourself a favor and explore the story of Dekanawida the Peacemaker, who a thousand years or so ago came among the warring Iroquois, united the nations, and created the Great Law of Peace, which influenced not only the American spirit of liberty and democracy, but also the United States Constitution – and governs the Iroquois to this day. This story should be imbedded in our civics curriculum.

THE GALLERY

"You cannot conquer America!" William Pitt declared. The words are writ large in our Declaration of Independence exhibit. (My brother-in-law Bill Aldhizer's wife Martha is a descendant of the Pitts, a fact which I learned long ago very soon after reading a biography of them and which helped to explain the Pitt-like streaks of creativity and insight she often displays, a remarkable genetic inheritance not uncommon in her family today.)

While managing what was clearly a rebellion, the First Continental Congress in 1774 and the Second Continental Congress in 1775 pursued a policy aimed at reconciliation with the Mother Country – reconciliation *with* equal rights – and in that spirit formally petitioned the Parliament. The majority party would not even officially accept the petitions. Wiser heads might have avoided what was coming, but there were stubborn men on both sides of the Atlantic, digging in their heels.

Loyalties were being tested, friendships strained, families divided. The rift between patriot Ben Franklin and his son William the royal governor of New Jersey would never be healed. The Crown Prince of England could be seen in the streets of London wearing the colors of the Continental Army in defiance of his father the King.

In 1776, frustrated by Parliament and inspired by Thomas Paine's powerful pamphlet "Common Sense," the Continental Congress ended the rebellion and formally started the American Revolution by declaring the independence of the United States of America.

* * *

Five words dominate our display. I ask my groups to say them: "All men are created equal." Say them again: "All men are created equal." How do you suppose those words sounded to the divinely anointed kings and tsars and emperors?

And what makes us think we can win this war? Who has the best army in the world? *They* do. We have mostly untrained militia. Who has the best navy in the world? *They* do. We don't have a single ship with guns. Who has a well organized government? *They* do. We have a weak committee by comparison. Who has more than three times as many people and a far greater advantage in industrial resources? Et cetera!

When those 56 men signed that declaration – a declaration of high treason in the view of some people – they were fully aware not only of the magnitude of their decision and its potential impact on the course of human history, but also of the odds stacked heavily against them.

Again I ask: What makes us think we can win this war? We do indeed have a righteous cause – Patrick Henry said that "righteousness alone will exalt us as a nation" – but that's not enough to win a war. Yes, we know the territory better (but so do the loyalists among us). And yes, in time, our new army and navy will mature and become respectable, we hope.

I summon forward a boy in my group, and ask his classmates to say "Good day, Jebediah." They do. Jebediah is my neighbor, serving alongside me in the Continental Army. Is he a good soldier? Not really, though he will become one. What (besides the omnipresent righteous cause) is he fighting for? His family, his home, his community, his reputation!

I call forward another boy, and ask his classmates to say "Guten tag, Heinrich." They do. Heinrich is a Hessian soldier, one of many serving with the British. Is he a good soldier? One of the best in the world. What is he fighting for? Money.

Whom do you want fighting alongside you?

Motivation is so important.

* * *

I ask my people if any of them have seen the "real" Declaration of Independence at the National Archives in Washington; often, some have; twice, groups had seen it days earlier. Most people are unaware that every night the Declaration of Independence and the Constitution and the Bill of Rights are lowered into an underground vault strong enough to protect them from the biggest bomb ever built. **That** is how precious they are – not just to Americans, but to all of humanity.

This is the time to ask my groups, particularly the people who have been to the National Archives, if they would like to see a copy of the Declaration *older* than what people see on display in

Washington. You bet they'd like to see it. So I show it to them – our copy of the Boston printing of the Declaration, done before the men gathered in Philadelphia to sign the formal document now in the National Archives.

I tell my groups to ask me how much this Boston printing cost (with donated funds) to purchase? They ask. I don't know, I say, but do note that a copy of the Boston printing sold at auction in 2009 for about $722,500; and that a copy of the earlier Philadelphia printing sold at auction in 2000 for $8.14 million. Yes, it is **that** precious, literally as well as figuratively.

Pop Quiz

How many women signed the Declaration of Independence? How many black people? How many Hispanics? Et cetera.

Why not?

That is why it's called a *continuing revolution* – a national promise to keep working at it until we get it right, whenever.

* * *

It took me a mighty long time – until only a few years ago, in fact – to comprehend fully and precisely why we **must** study history: It's to learn how to make good decisions!

130

In the "witnesses" section, where we tell the stories of real people and the choices they faced, I focus on four men – the merchant who remained loyal to the crown, and lost everything; the Mohawk chief who declared the neutrality of his people, and was jailed for it; the slave who, for his freedom and the greater cause, fought for independence; and the slave who, for his freedom, fought against it. (By the end of the war, one in seven soldiers in the Continental Army was black. Thousands of blacks fought alongside or in other ways supported the British.)

I ask a student if he or she has made any decisions today. "Yes," he or she answers. "There!" I declare. "That was a decision! Every word you say, every deliberate motion you make, is a decision. You make hundreds, maybe thousands, of decisions every day. Most of the decisions you'll need to make in life will be trivial, but some will be important, and a few will be *really* important. So be prepared to make good decisions. Study history."

Why, exactly? Because life is all about decisions, and history is a classroom for studying how human beings have dealt with various situations and problems and crises and opportunities, how and why they decided what to do, and what were the consequences of those decisions.

One of our great weaknesses in education today is our foolish neglect of critical thinking as a vital component of any curriculum. In the absence of any other remedy, I say: Study more history!

* * *

Marie-Joseph Paul Yves Roch Gilbert du Motier, Marquis de La Fayette (later just Citizen Lafayette) was among the many Europeans who came to America to offer their services to the insurgent cause.

Motivated by a zeal for liberty, Lafayette was 19. Washington was initially not very impressed. They became like father and son.

Our display includes a formal portrait of Lafayette, a pair of pistols once his, and an 18th century illustration of the general at Yorktown, standing next to his horse, the horse's reins held by a black man wearing flamboyant red livery, a European conception of the moment. I tell my groups that there is a school in my community named Lafayette High, then ask them for whom the school is named – the European nobleman, or an African slave . . . or both. Here I must tell a personal story.

What's in a Name?

In 1973, the joint school system of the City of Williamsburg and James City County was about to open a new high school, the first new school to serve our white and black people equally.

After much discussion and indecision about what to name it – Pocahontas, maybe, or Chanco or Lafayette or whatever – the School Board asked for public comments. So I commented in a letter to the superintendent, strongly recommending that the school be named Lafayette, to honor equally the European nobleman who served the Revolution so well (both here and in Europe) and the obscure African slave who served as the master spy of Yorktown – James Armistead, who later obtained his freedom with the help of Lafayette and changed his name to James Armistead Lafayette. I wrote that naming the school Lafayette would be an ideal way to serve the continuing American Revolution on the eve of the Bicentennial.

The superintendent liked the letter and asked permission to share it with members of the School Board. I said sure.

At the School Board's next regular meeting, the eagerly awaited decision was made to name it – !!! – the Williamsburg-James City County High School. A brief article in the morning newspaper announced it. And bright and early that morning, the students and teachers and staff at James Blair High began rising with virtual unanimity in an open rebellion which quickly spread to Berkeley Middle. Education ground to a halt, and a petition signed by just about everybody at both schools told the School

Board that education would not resume until they changed the name of the new school.

That night, in special session, the School Board capitulated, and told the students at both schools to choose the name.

After a proper discussion and election, they chose Lafayette. Today, formal portraits of the two Lafayettes adorn the school's entrance lobby. Power to the people!

It is one of the finer footnotes to the modern history of the greater Williamsburg community that the 1973 Lafayette High football team (which under ordinary circumstances might have gone 6-4) went 12-1, yielding only six touchdowns and losing only in the state championship game – the best high school football team I've ever seen, a model of teamwork, spirit, discipline and execution, a joy to watch. Graduates of that 1970s golden era in the history of the Lafayette Rams include NFL notables Mel Gray, Ron Springs and, oh yes, Lawrence Taylor, arguably the greatest defensive player in the history of football.

* * *

I've suggested a new illustration for our Lafayette exhibit: Lafayette in his command tent on the day after the formal surrender, when British officers, accordant with the courtesies of the day, came to pay their respects – their faces in amazement at the sight of the man standing next to Lafayette and wearing not flamboyant red livery but the uniform of the Continental Army – James Armistead, the faithful slave who for months had served them so well, so well indeed that they asked him to be a spy for them, which he was of course happy to do.

Spy *and* counterspy. Great story. It would make a great movie, and someday probably will.

Footnote: In 1824, toward the beginning of Lafayette's triumphal tour of the United States, he and his spy met again in Yorktown.

* * *

I pause at the Constitution section, and ask my groups to say the words which dominate it. "We the People." Say them again. "We the People."

Once, a whole class of middle schoolers didn't wait for the second request, but proceeded to recite, with meaning, the whole preamble. Terrific!

It is said that the only thing which united the colonies – their Englishness – is the thing against which they rebelled; that if they had not gone to war with the Mother Country, eventually they would have gone to war among themselves. We forget nowadays just how distinct each colony was in its culture, economy, demographics, climate. You would *never* mistake a Massachusetts man for a

New York man, or a South Carolinian for a Georgian, or a Virginian for a Marylander. No way.

Patrick Henry said: "I am not a Virginian. I am an American." But there were many not so quick to embrace the new concept.

The colonies won their independence and became uneasy partners in a loose confederation of still largely sovereign states. It was an impractical arrangement.

The extraordinary convention of 1787 – Catherine Drinker Bowen's **Miracle at Philadelphia** tells the story superbly – produced the world's first written national constitution, a model for humanity.

And what were its first words?

* * *

Most people have never heard of the Betsy, one of the supply ships scuttled by the British during the siege, or of the archaeologist John Broadwater. But most people have heard of the USS Monitor, excavated by a team led by John, who mastered underwater archaeology in the York River with the Betsy.

We have a fine exhibit of artifacts from the Betsy, most of them everyday items attesting to the simple humanity of the crew.

* * *

Actually, my favorite teaching point in this section has almost nothing to do with the Betsy.

We have a video screen showing a 1781 French map of Yorktown and immediate vicinity. Press a button, and the screen shows an aerial view of Yorktown. You can see our museum, and the pier where the Betsy was excavated – and if you look closely you can see a certain brick house with two chimneys, the finest old house in Yorktown.

Preparing for the great bombardment, the American gunners asked their commander where to sight their guns, to get the range. He pointed to that prominent house, a logical target – and today you can see cannonballs still imbedded in the side of the house of General Thomas Nelson, Signer of the Declaration, who fully supported the order to fire on it and even offered a cash prize to the first gunners to hit it!

THE ENCAMPMENT

Before entering the camp, it is appropriate to tell, at least briefly, the story of what happened at Yorktown, to try to explain why what happened here was and is so very important.

Late in 1780, the military situation was bright for the British and bleak for the Americans, to say the least.

The British army and navy based in New York City were too strong to be engaged by Washington's

Continental Army even with their new allies the French, commanded by the Comte de Rochambeau. The rebel cause to the south was dealt a devastating blow in South Carolina in May of '80, when General Henry Clinton forced the surrender of General Benjamin Lincoln's army of more than 5,200 men at Charleston. (To make it worse, Clinton denied Lincoln's brave men the traditional honors of war, an act of scorn and humiliation.)

Early in 1781, Washington privately conceded that the war was probably lost, that it would take a miracle to win it. "We are at the end of our tether," he said. "Now or never our deliverance must come."

* * *

During the summer of '81, badly pestered by the rebels but still dominant, Charles Cornwallis entrenched his army of about 7,500 British and Hessian soldiers in and around the port of Yorktown and across the York River at Gloucester Point. A prosperous village, Yorktown was a major port of exit for Virginia tobacco and a major port of entry for African slaves. It was a secure position, with a strong British fleet commanding the Chesapeake.

Call it a miracle or merely miraculous, what happened next was by common-sense definition a high-risk, high-stakes gamble, an all-in bet. For the Americans, failure probably meant defeat, and a negotiated peace dictated by Parliament; success probably meant victory, a political as well as military defeat for the parliamentary majority in a nation tired of a costly, controversial civil war. Whatever the end to this war, it would affect the course of human history, and people everywhere knew it.

* * *

To appreciate the magnitude of the risk and boldness required to make it happen, be very mindful of the methods, speed and unreliability of communications at the time.

Learning that a French fleet commanded by the Comte de Grasse was in the Caribbean, Rochambeau dispatched a message to de Grasse.

Then, early in September, not knowing when or even if the message would arrive, the American and French armies stunningly abandoned their positions at New York and began streaming south. (As word of the movement of the armies became known and it became apparent where they were heading, there was widespread religious amazement that perhaps the final decisive battle of this vital war would be fought within a dozen miles of Jamestown – and Williamsburg – where it all began. It is a remarkable fact.)

Washington knew the war was probably won well before he reached Yorktown. En route, he learned that de Grasse had gotten the message and

139

had brought his fleet to the Chesapeake. Boyishly eager to share the news with Rochambeau, Washington went onto a river pier with his hat in one hand and a handkerchief in the other, dancing up and down, shouting the news to the arriving French commander – a scene I want on the back of the $1 bill. A French officer observed that Washington looked like a child whose every wish had come true.

* * *

It would be a siege, and the French were the best siege engineers in the world.

While Cornwallis and his men dug in, waiting for the relief fleet which never came, the American and French armies on the 28th of September began to arrive and move into position. Skirmishing began.

On the 9th of October, the heavy allied bombardment (and the heavy British response) began, continuing night and day until the 17th, when the British awoke to discover a much tighter siege line – and the presence of newly arrived large naval guns from the French fleet. With Yorktown already in ruins and many of its defenders too ill or wounded to be of any service, the future was predictable.

Diane Smith

George Washington

The end had come. The white flag of truce appeared. The guns stopped firing – and wherever the suddenly awesome silence could be heard, people knew what it meant.

On Friday the 19th of October 1781, following the signing of the document of surrender at the Moore House, the men of Lord Cornwallis – denied the honors of war in retaliation for Charleston – filed out of their positions at Yorktown, onto what is now known as the Surrender Road, to what is now known as Surrender Field, their way on either side lined by the men of Washington and Rochambeau. Cornwallis, essentially blameless but properly mortified by the defeat, stayed behind, indisposed, requiring his second-in-command, General Charles O'Hara, to lead the procession.

Arriving at the field, O'Hara offered his sword to Rochambeau, who declined it, motioning to Washington, who declined it, motioning to his second-in-command, who accepted it, then honorably returned it. That man was Benjamin (note well the last name) Lincoln.

When the news of Yorktown reached London, Lord Frederick North the Prime Minister declared: "Oh God, it's all over."

And the eminent Horace Walpole observed: "From the hour that fatal egg, the Stamp Act, was laid, I disliked it and all the vipers hatched from it."

It is a tragic but I think necessary footnote that the garrison captured at Charleston was transported to New York and put on the infamous prison ships, where by the time of the Treaty of Paris in 1783 more than 6,000 American prisoners of war died, including most of the men from Charleston.

* * *

More often than not, as our encampment suggests, armies back then were not fighting – either in open battle, from time to time, from place to place, one army trying to force another army off the field; or in concentrated siege, one (usually larger) army surrounding another army, cutting off its supplies and hopes of escape, forcing it to surrender. What happened at Yorktown was, I repeat, a siege.

Most of the time, the army was in camp or on the march, constantly foraging, training, killing time, making ready for battle, whenever and wherever it might come.

This encampment displays "housing" ranging from the common soldiers' small tents (as many as six men per tent at times) to the necessarily much larger colonel's tent, a punishment area, a quartermaster's tent with nearby field kitchen, a site where women (soldiers' wives) traveling with the army would do laundry and sewing for the men, a medical station and the area reserved for regular demonstrations of the firing of a flintlock musket, or a mortar, or a field cannon – the echo of each firing resounding from across a swampy ravine, reinforcing the effect. I wonder if there will be an echo in the camp's eventual new location.

Entering the colonel's tent, casually picking up and playing with a quill pen, I ask my groups to find the potty and the computer. The chamber pot is easily found, under the cot. The computer proves elusive – not that book, no, not that desk – until someone finally notices the quill pen I now hold atop my head. Time to talk about then and now. Then, a horseman riding from Yorktown to Williamsburg with an urgent message might need several hours to get there – in daylight and good weather. Now, I can and sometimes do hit the send tab and say hello to a friend in Chelyabinsk, Russia, in less than a second.

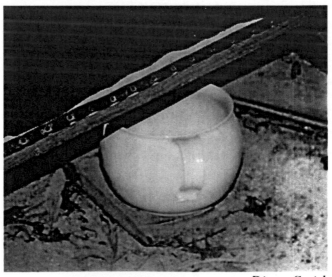

Diane Smith

The potty

Diane Smith

The computer

* * *

The medical station, a display of instruments and pharmacy bottles, is an excellent place to discuss the progress of humanity, in real and relevant terms.

While it's true that any quack with a trepanning tool and a really stupid patient could claim to be a brain surgeon, did they have any good doctors in 1781? Yes, there were many fine medical schools in Europe and two in America, so there were many very good doctors, up to a point. Human beings have been trying and learning how to cure what ails us for thousands of years, accumulating great stores of knowledge about the human body, pharmacology, the symptoms and sorts of illness, treating burns and rashes and fevers and broken bones, performing complex surgery with instruments very much like the ones used by ancient Greek and Roman doctors.

But there was no effective anesthetic, except the loss of consciousness; forget about alcohol, which might make you oblivious to reality but would also increase the flow of your blood, bad in a tooth extraction, maybe fatal in surgery. And nobody knew what a germ was! The sad fact is that a majority of the men wounded in combat during that war, and many other past wars, died not from their wounds but literally at the hands of their doctors and nurses, men (there being no women doctors or nurses) doing their best to relieve pain and save lives with unwashed hands and unsterilized instruments invisibly spreading disease and infection.

Sometimes, I ask students to smile for me. Kids love to smile. Then I ask them if they've heard about George Washington's teeth. Many have. Somehow, it has become the subject of laughter in our culture. It wasn't funny to Mr. Washington, who when he became president had only one of his original teeth left and lost that one during his second term. Throughout his adult life, increasingly he needed false teeth, clumsy contraptions by modern standards; the man could not speak as well, eat as well, smile as well. (One day, with a group of fifth-graders from northern Virginia, I routinely asked if they had heard about George Washington's teeth. Well, in the next few minutes I learned more about Mr. Washington's teeth than I ever aspired to know; I was wowed. I learned that day either **never** to ask a class from Mt. Vernon Elementary School in Fairfax about George Washington's teeth; or **always** ask 'em, so they can have the joy of teaching me.)

* * *

When I had to wear a partial cast on my right forearm after surgery to reattach a severed tendon in my index finger, I was asked what had happened, creating a teaching moment.

Here's what happened:

In frustration, I had rashly reached inside a hubcap and yanked it, immediately feeling a sharp twinge inside my palm. Then and there, God spoke to me. She said: "Son, I can abide ignorance. But stupidity you gotta pay for." Hence, surgery to repair the tendon and restore the flexibility of my finger; hence, too, the cast. (The surgery didn't work, but I don't mind; in fact, I'm thankful for the stupid accident. It reminded me of lessons I supposedly had already learned about anger, patience and the characteristics of good decision-making.)

147

Then there's my nose.

For a month or so, there was a tiny circular bandaid on the left side of my nose. Some kids asked me about it, so I explained it. By the time the last bandaid came off – after one doctor's advanced dermatology procedure and then 45 minutes of cosmetic surgery by a team of two doctors and three nurses to make my nose beautiful again – I had some good questions to ask my groups:

"When I was told I had a skin cancer on my nose, was I scared?" Yes! "No, not at all. I know about this type of cancer and what a good doctor can do to cure it. So I wasn't scared in the least.

"Later, when I was on the operating table, surrounded by doctors and nurses, was I asleep?" Yes! "No, I was wide awake. My eyes were covered, but that didn't stop all of us from having a great conversation and some good laughs. Twice, one of the doctors said something which prompted me to ask the nurses: 'Does he really know what he's doing?' The first time, a nurse replied: 'We guess so.' The second time, another nurse replied: 'We sure hope so.' A good time was had by all – and my nose *is* beautiful again. Actually, it's not a very pretty nose, but it's the only one I've got, so you can understand my close attachment to it."

* * *

Today, we know what a germ is – and DNA.

We can anaesthetize all or a small part of a person.

We can determine where a cavity *will be* and prevent it from beginning.

The average well trained nurse knows more than most of the doctors of the 18th century. I myself, with a veterinarian's guidance, have provided more advanced medical care to my pets at home than I myself might have received in the 18th century at the best hospital in the world.

Young people today have never heard of polio, a terrifying scourge when I was a child. Would you like to hear about my recent *very* brief but spectacularly successful cataract surgery? Et cetera, et cetera, et cetera. I wish we had time to talk about the future of nanotechnology in medicine; I'd love to learn more about it.

* * *

One final observation before leaving the encampment: One day, a pleasant lady covered her ears and advised me to cover my ears just before a musket firing. I told her it was too late to be careful, that I had set off too many cherry-bombs and firecrackers in my youth (or so an audiologist once told me).

"Cover your ears," she calmly persisted. Sensing my continued resistance, she said, nicely but sternly, still covering her ears: "I worked in an audiologist's office. Your hearing can be damaged even more. Cover your ears." I meekly did. Good advice. Are you listening?

(Now hear this as well: Open your mouth, too. The danger of a loud noise is its concussive effect, which is why sticking your fingers in your ears is not a good idea; in fact, it increases the danger.)

B AND PATRICK HENRY

I do not hide my profound admiration of Mr. Henry; indeed, I proclaim it. Sometimes, I even refer to him as "a personal friend of mine" . . . which requires some explanation.

As a sophomore at the College of William and Mary in 1960, I wrote the script for a costumed re-enactment of the Stamp Act debate on the 30th of May 1765, presented in the Capitol to a gathering of collegiate debaters. I was Patrick Henry.

Later, as a teacher of public speaking and coach of forensics at Walsingham Academy for seven years, I always had a Patrick Henry in the competition, and he always did well. My best Patrick Henry, Paul Maxfield, had exactly the type of musically appealing voice I am convinced Patrick Henry must have had, to be so mesmerizing. Jefferson wrote: "When he had spoken in opposition

Tom Williams

B as Patrick Henry in 1960

to my opinion, had produced a great effect, and I myself been highly delighted and moved, I have asked myself when he ceased: What the d---l has he said?" (Henry had a sister whose voice reportedly could be heard distinctly at a distance of more than a mile. Think about the type of voice required to do that.)

In 1972, I wrote a book of poetry focusing on that great historical event – **the 30th of may: a poem of the revolution**. Later that year, in adaptation as "Williamsburg: Window of the Revolution," it was broadcast on public radio in Philadelphia as a two-hour dramatic production, in which I read the part of Henry.

In 1989, I wrote **Mabel and Mr. Henry,** a memoir of Mabel Oliver Bellwood, the remarkable lady who rescued from ruin Mr. Henry's beloved final home and resting place at Red Hill. Doing research, I went to Red Hill, and was permitted to hold the letter opener which Henry held in 1775 during his fateful declaration: "Give me liberty or give me death!"

* * *

Then there's the matter of Mr. Henry's interference in the life of two of my ancestors, the one he put at risk of treason, the prosperous Benjamin Clement; and the one he got out of jail, the poor John Weatherford.

The latter was a Baptist dissenter who stubbornly insisted on his right to preach the gospel wherever and whenever the spirit moved him, without a license from the Anglican authorities. He was therefore jailed in Chesterfield County for several months (a good story in itself) until his considerable fines were paid anonymously by Patrick Henry.

Twenty years or so later, Weatherford learned who had paid his fines and sent a small amount of money in token payment to Henry at Red Hill; the Voice of the Revolution returned it.

Weatherford is among the most notable of the so-called Baptist Martyrs of Virginia during colonial times – also known, more accurately, as the Imprisoned Baptist Ministers of Virginia, since none of them died in the course of persecution.

Footnote: When I was growing up, I didn't know about Clement or Weatherford – or about the ancestor who received the first gubernatorial pardon for a capital crime (killing a judge's nephew in a barroom brawl) in Virginia history after serving the longest time in prison (for a white man) in Virginia history – or about the ancestor who served in Kemper's Brigade of Pickett's Division. Fortunately, my lawyer-cousins Kenneth Dobyns on my mother's side and Pete Joyner on my father's side did the genealogical research. Thanks, guys. (When Ken told me about Weatherford, he said it explained the stubborn streak in me.)

Footnote to the footnote: Another ancestor sold all of his property in Virginia, converting it into a purseful of money, then deposited his family with kinfolk while he journeyed westward to find new land. Overnighting at a tavern with other travelers, he went to sleep with his purse beneath his pillow; in the morning, the purse was empty. He returned to Virginia, and started from scratch, thus enabling me to be here writing this. It's an odd feeling, owing one's existence to a long-ago thief in the night.

Plus: As a consequence of writing this book, I very recently learned more about the family tree of Benjamin Clement – grandson of Jeremiah Clement, who at the age of nine sailed with his siblings and their widowed mother, Lady Elizabeth Clement, on the ship George from London to Jamestown in 1616. Jeremiah's father, Sir Jeffrey Clement, was a prominent London merchant, a shareholder in the Virginia Company and an investor in a shipping company which brought many of the early settlers to Virginia. One of the ships was the George, which on its return voyage in 1616 carried Pocahontas et al to England.

Elizabeth must have been a remarkable woman, coming here with her children so early in the Virginia adventure. When I try to imagine what she and Jeremiah experienced – the danger, the opportunity, the people they encountered, the history in which they participated – I feel stronger, somehow, more deeply rooted, more confident that I have been and am on the right path in life.

According to the Clement family genealogy, a great-great-grandson of Benjamin was Samuel Langhorne Clemens, also known as Mark Twain.

* * *

Finally, I note the day a few years ago when I was in the downtown post office and a man in handsome colonial attire got into line behind me. I asked him: "Who, sir, might you be?"

"I, sir," he said, "am Patrick Henry, of Hanover County."

So I offered him my hand in thanks for getting my ancestor out of jail. Oh yes, he remembered that case well. Then I chided him for inducing another ancestor to make gunpowder. He didn't know about that gentleman, so I enlightened him. He seemed pleased to learn about it.

So, in a sense, you see, I am at least a personal acquaintance of Mr. Henry. (I refer to Richard Schumann, Colonial Williamsburg's impressive Henry. I subsequently shared with him a copy of **the 30th of may**, as I had previously shared a copy with Bill Barker, CW's inimitable Jefferson.)

So what signifies <u>wishing</u> and <u>hoping</u>
for better times . . . We may <u>make</u>
these times better if we bestir ourselves.
Benjamin Franklin

CHAPTER 4: PEOPLE AT WORK

AN INTERESTING ILK

I cannot successfully and therefore shall not vainly attempt to recognize all of the many co-workers, past and present in a constantly changing cast of characters, who have made my time with the Jamestown-Yorktown Foundation so interesting and wonderful.

Frankly, my biggest worry in writing this book is the absence from it of many of my dearest friends, who simply have not done or said anything sufficiently outrageous and/or funny and/or instructive to merit inclusion, at least not that I can remember. To these excluded friends I say: You're not in the book, but you're still in my heart.

When I told Rosemary Rankin in Visitor Services that I was writing this book, she glanced up from her computer long enough to say she was very glad to hear it. When I told her that she wasn't in the book yet, she casually said, without glancing up from her computer: "Oh, that's all right. I will be." And she's right. I could not in good conscience write this book and omit Rosemary, my steadfast companion in worrying – with hope – about the nation and the world and the future. We have strengthened one another's faith.

I must mention veteran MPA Barbara Laroche, who was a student of mine at Walsingham Academy more years ago than either of us cares to count, a cheerleader who always cheered me up then and is my cheerleader today. It made me very happy when she introduced herself to me on the loop many years ago. It was a reassuring sign that I was in the right place, somehow.

Because they have done and daily do so much to make this place what it is, I shall also make special mention of my most relevant bosses, all really good people – Phil Emerson, executive director; Anne Price-Hardister, director of the on-site education program; and Karen Norako, Lynn DeVito and Sandy Key, assistant education officers, the good-natured ladies who directly administer the MPAs and control the occasional chaos.

* * *

In the office, amid the early clamor of a busy day, some MPAs began wondering aloud why they came to work here. Marilyn Conley piped up: "Bill came here because it's a great place to meet babes!"

Much laughter. No argument, Marilyn being one of the best of 'em.

One day, I overheard a student telling another: "The people who work here sure do laugh a lot!"

* * *

Twice, my job performance has been "recognized" at staff meetings I was unable to attend:

- For frequently coming to the rescue to substitute for ill or otherwise missing MPAs, I received the modest but symbolically important "Life-Saver Award," a pack of life-savers — which I never got, because **somebody** ate 'em!

- Karen Norako reported that I had "walked on water" in dealing with a weekend group of home school children and adults. This is what happened that Saturday morning (very early in the museum's effort to attract home school groups): This "group" pre-registered 17 students, with a unknown number of adults to be expected. Instead, about 15 different groups arrived at about 15 different times, requiring me to dash back and forth finding and rallying my people and leaving messages for late arrivals where to find us. The group finally started out, late but intact, with more than 17 home schoolers, plus siblings ranging in age from infancy to college, plus mothers and fathers and aunts and uncles and grandparents – a total of 51, as I vaguely recall. Might've been more.

* * *

Many individual students (and adults) and some whole groups come here especially hungry for knowledge and understanding, and especially appreciative when I try to feed them generously, expanding and intensifying my teaching, helping them to know more and think better.

With one such group in the village, I walked over to where Duane Baldwin, who speaks Lakota Sioux, was working on a deer hide. I told him I had a really good group and wanted to reward them with something special, and asked if he would mind speaking a few words in Lakota. Instead, he told my people about a song written by an imprisoned Lakota – and then sang it! My people and I were enthralled. Bravo, Duane!!!

* * *

I must tell you about interpreter Don Hulick, a longtime hugging companion. He's a former Navy man, and I suppose I should take with a grain of salt some of the stories he tells. But he tells such great stories. Sometimes, I share them briefly with my groups before or after they meet him; sometimes, at my bidding, he tells them himself; sometimes, we tell them together.

He parachuted out of two crashing airplanes, but went all the way down with a helicopter, fusing his spine, shortening him by an inch and a half. The painful part, he said, was being stretched back out.

He fell off the flight deck of an aircraft carrier at sea, recovering consciousness to watch his home moving away from him at about 30 knots. He suffered one bruise, from the top of his head to the tips of his toes. Thus, he became the star of a Navy film on flight deck safety. He never saw the film. Didn't want to. Been there, done that.

He was in another Navy film, about cold weather operations. He's been to the South Pole 37 times. Doesn't plan to go back. It's cold down there!

"I'm a survivor," he says.

And a mighty fine interpreter and friend as well.

* * *

If while leading a tour you do something the procedures say you're not supposed to do, you can be "written up" – reported to the higher authorities. It's necessary, I suppose. Rules *are* rules, and excellence *is* in the details. But it can be annoying sometimes, because sometimes there really are two sides to a story. I've been written up a few times.

Diane Smith

**Don Hulick and Duane Baldwin aboard
the Susan Constant with the old Godspeed
across the cove**

I can recall the first time. For some reason, I stopped my group (briefly but wrongly) just outside the entrance to the old gallery, came inside, exchanged smiles with two Visitor Services ladies, then promptly stopped (briefly but wrongly) at the imposing statue of Powhatan rather than walk right past it with only a fleeting reference, then proceeded. A few minutes later, we were approached by Susan Mahady of Visitor Services, a usually good-humored English lady, who apologized for interrupting me, then sternly told me I was being written up. She produced a washroom paper towel, and read from it: "Bill write up . . . Stopping in front of doors. Entering front doors. Stopping at Powhatan . . . Susan & Louise." With a smiley face! I love it!

* * *

Master interpreter Jim Harrison and I have been hugging for many years, whenever we meet on site, sometimes twice a day when I have two tours, sometimes twice on a single tour. We enjoy hugging.

Jim has a witty way of engaging groups, during interpretations and when he invites a student or adult to pose comically with him while others take photographs. People love Jim.

One busy day, an idle conversation enriched the meaning of our hugs. Leading my group onto the Susan but stalled at the top of the gangway, I mentioned to Jim that I had just learned that one of our co-workers had an ancestor who came to Virginia in 1622, adding that the first Bryant didn't arrive until 1631.

"Well," Jim said, "my people came later . . . but I dare say they were a better class of people."

"Indeed, sir," I said with a certain formality indicating maybe I should be offended. "And who, sir, were your people?"

"My people, sir," he said with an equally certain air of dignity, "were the Pages of Rosewell, and the Harrisons of Brandon."

Like a proper yeoman in the presence of gentry, I bowed deferentially in his direction. "Definitely," I quite agreed, "a better class of people."

Then we hugged, and I proceeded with my group.

Since then, after one of my groups has met Jim, I gather my people and ask: "Do you like Jim?" They do. "Did you notice I hugged him?" They did. "Do you know why I hugged him?" Not really. "Because I love him . . . and because when I hug Jim I know I'm hugging a descendant of someone who probably hugged Thomas Jefferson – John Page, Jefferson's closest friend.

Not to mention that Jim is also descended from two presidents of the United States."

Sometimes, I note that Jim was in the Navy for 20 years. Seal Team 3.

People feel honored to meet him.

* * *

Ordinarily, I should say routinely, in everything from planting pretty flowers and mowing the lawn to keeping our restrooms immaculate (something visitors comment on), the folks in buildings and grounds maintenance do a splendid job in making us look good not only to our visitors, but also to ourselves, which is important. I cannot praise those folks enough.

Sometimes, however, a message doesn't reach the right person; or if it does, it isn't taken seriously enough. Example: The sign.

The reconstruction of Jamestown Settlement transformed the landscape, creating not only a great new building, but also new designated parking areas for employees, general visitors and buses.

But there was a problem: A sign had been posted on Jamestown Road pointing buses to proceed straight ahead (to the new bus area) and cars to turn left (to the new visitor area) – but the sign was much too small, and it was in the wrong place.

The problem became obvious (at least to the MPAs) as soon as the busy season began in the spring of 2006, as bus driver after bus driver after bus driver made the long-accustomed left turn and promptly became confused, hesitantly entering the visitor area, trying to figure out where to go, eventually either finding the crosslane between the two areas or being directed to it by a frantically waving MPA dashing to the rescue. It was a mess, particularly in the busy season.

The bus drivers certainly weren't at fault. But we figured that each such delay cost us – and by us I mean the MPAs, the students, the teachers – *at least* five minutes of precious teaching and learning time (multiplied by however many people were on the bus), not a trivial matter for people on tight schedules. Several MPAs reported the problem and asked that it be fixed, soon. What happened to the message next isn't known.

The sign

Well, the problem wasn't fixed. The problem continued to the end of the busy spring season, and resumed at the beginning of the busy autumn season. Clearly, something had to be done. So I did it.

One morning, I took a Polaroid photograph of the existing sign, went to Kinko's, had the photo enlarged and laminated, then returned to the Settlement, and, with some duct tape, firmly affixed the new sign over the old one. This had been accomplished in about an hour at a cost of less than $3.

No problem.

* * *

At a general meeting of MPAs, Lynn DeVito invited us to play a game. She would cite an interesting fact in the life of an MPA, and we would guess the person's identity.

First test: "I spent six weeks living with a Moroccan family on the grounds of the King's palace in Rabat."

"Bill Bryant!" someone blurted out, to the mild amusement of my colleagues.

"No," Lynn said, "not Bill Bryant." (The right ID: Laurin Wittig.)

Second test: "I was at a nearby Chinese restaurant when the Berlin Wall fell."

"Bill Bryant!" someone shouted, to much laughter, in the midst of which I heard one MPA say to another: "Well, that would certainly explain it."

"Now," Lynn said as the laughter subsided, "you can't answer 'Bill Bryant' every time!" (The right ID: Suzanne Gainey.)

If I had been asked to submit a clue for that game, I thought at the time, I probably would have rejected the simple "I slept one night in the Coliseum in Rome" or the interesting "I had breakfast with Johnny Unitas" in favor of the more provocative "When I first met and hugged Jessie Jackson I was wearing a suit and tie and he was wearing only jockey shorts." True story; amusing, too, but long ago and not relevant to this book.

What begins to approach relevance is that one day Jessie led his entourage, then (in the mid-1970s) including me, down to Lafayette Square to picket against apartheid in front of the White House. My work with him at the time focused on inner-city education, and I didn't want to get involved with anything of a partisan political nature, but I could see no harm in it. On site, with what I thought was an unnecessarily heavy police (and I assume FBI) presence nearby, Jessie handed me a sign. It said: Free Mandela. I picketed, in honest opposition to apartheid but with only a vague idea of who Mandela was.

What is arguably relevant is that on several occasions I have encountered South African students on my tours. I have asked that if he or she ever happened to meet Mr. Mandela, to tell him that Bill Bryant of Virginia loves him and would kiss his feet if given the opportunity . . . Rest in peace, Madiba.

* * *

One day in the village, Frank Hardister and I were talking about the cast of "unusual" characters with whom we worked. "Let's face it, Bill," he said. "Who else would hire *us*?"

When I shared this witticism with MPA Norm Fuss, he laughed. "We *are* an unusual bunch of characters – and that's one of the best things about working at this place. We are **not** plain vanilla!"

* * *

On two memorable occasions at Yorktown, Norm has stolen the spotlight from me, not as an MPA but as a tall and imposing 18th century soldier – in opposing armies!

One day on the farm, Norm entered the scene wearing the handsome uniform of an infantry private in the Continental Army. He stopped to chat with my group, the chat quickly developing into a marvelous discussion of his uniform, of the life of a soldier, of the virtuous cause for which he was fighting. My students were spellbound. So was I. It was the best costumed interpretation I had ever seen . . . though not for long.

Some months later, approaching the entrance to the gallery, I and my group encountered Norm and his MPA wife Barbara – he wearing the splendid red uniform of a captain in the British Army's Corps of Engineers, she wearing the equally splendid red uniform of the captain's wife. They were an elegant couple. Soon, fully in character, he engaged my group, making them think, vigorously challenging the viewpoint of the American rebels, with equal vigor asserting the merits of being a British citizen and the virtue of the cause for which he was fighting – with such convincing logic that I felt I should lead my group away, lest he contaminate their impressionable young minds.

Well done, Norm!

Diane Smith

Greg Schneck at work in the garden

Footnote: While applauding one co-worker for stealing my spotlight, I might as well applaud a couple of others who have abruptly stolen it quite conspicuously – fort interpreter Fred Scholpp, who, without asking, simply commandeered my school group (after the tour was basically over), armed them with wooden weapons, and put them through

10 minutes of training, to their great delight; and farm interpreter Greg Schneck, who, as I led my school group into the vegetable garden for a brief walk-through glimpse, not only began explaining a display of freshly picked vegetables, but also then directed the youngsters to another interpreter, who put them to work planting three rows of seeds, a 10-minute delay, for planting good memories. What Norm and Fred and Greg did was to be themselves – teachers looking for students, even somebody else's!

* * *

Several MPAs began deploying on the patio, awaiting other MPAs leading several busloads of elementary school children in our direction. All was calm, for the moment.

One MPA, a lady of great dignity and decency, walked over to the edge of the patio and, with her back to the incoming storm of youngsters, surveyed the great lawn, and said, to no one in particular: "And we shall lead the little children out onto the field . . . and there we shall slay them."

* * *

On the final day of an especially grueling busy season in June of 2010, most of the MPAs gathered for a brief staff session and a pot-luck buffet.

Anne Price-Hardister began with a typically generous and heartfelt thanks to the MPAs for a job well done under often difficult conditions. Then she asked how many of us had done at least 10 tours during the busy season. All of us raised our hands. How many had done at least 20? Fewer hands. At least 30? Fewer hands. At least 40? Far fewer hands. At least 50? Only two people raised their hands – I and Barbara Rooney, sitting next to me. Anne then announced that in fact Barbara had done 76 tours, and I had done 82.

I leaned toward Barbara, who leaned toward me, and our foreheads met.

"No wonder we're so tired," I muttered.

Subsequently, I'm proud to say, Barbara and I shared the distinction of being the first MPAs ever recognized as Employees of the Quarter.

(A disclaimer: I had done only 81 tours. My tour that morning had been canceled.)

* * *

Before 2007, I was walking toward my car when I noticed fort interpreter Ralph Grimsley standing in a deep, wide, freshly dug construction ditch in front of the Settlement, where a new parking lot was taking shape.

I wandered over to the edge of one end of the ditch, and, knowing the answer, asked: "What are you doing down there?"

Instead of the answer I expected – searching for artifacts – Ralph began to opine, with unspoken but obvious reference to the 1781 skirmish fought somehwre near here: "The British," he said, looking and gesturing to his left, "were lined up about where that treeline is, and the French," he continued, looking and gesturing to his right, "would have been deployed over there, so I figure," he added, now looking and pointing his finger at the bottom of the ditch, slowing raising his hand, "that the Great Road must have been right about here," he concluded, his finger pointing at my feet.

According to Ralph's well educated guess, I was standing atop the Great Road!

"Found any artifacts?"

"No . . . not yet."

* * *

I didn't witness it, but I heard about it the next day from an MPA who was there: At the ships, with a group of students sitting on the pier in front of him, interpreter Steve Martin with a rope in his hands called for volunteers to learn how to tie a knot. He deliberately chose a boy with only one arm. And he taught that boy how to tie a knot! The boy, I was told, was joyful amid the applause of his classmates.

The same day I heard about it, I encountered Steve on the pier. I told him what I had heard, then hugged him, and (with difficulty 'cause he's a tall guy) planted a little kiss on his cheek. And that was all that really needed to be said and done. It's true that virtue is its own reward, but sometimes it's nice to honor it in other ways.

* * *

Exiting my favorite yehakin one day, I saw three interpreters – Steve Phillips, Duane Baldwin and Frank Hardister – at a cooking site, beginning to try to make fire without a match or a lighter, the Stone Age way. So I took my group over to them for a seldom seen demonstration.

Squatting, Steve tried hard, making a little smoke but no fire. So he got up and Duane replaced him, trying hard, making a little smoke but no fire. So he got up and Frank replaced him . . . and soon there was much smoke and a glowing ember, which he quickly transferred to a large tuft of kindling – and there was fire! (Made the old-fashioned way, by earning it.)

Amid the delight of the group, I just had to ask: "How many Indians does it take to start a fire?"

Duane instantly answered: "One Indian . . . three interpreters."

* * *

Like the making of history itself, the writing of this book has been a matter of reaching ever deeper into memory, seeking the details, the scenes, the themes, the people who have made this book worth writing.

And believe me, it hasn't been easy. A year ago, I absolutely did not intend to write another book. Some people think that writing must be fun. Not always, especially not with "serious" writing. The *having written* is fun; the writing itself can be, as my preacher-poet cousin Billy Joyner once said, velvet torture. (The beautiful Helen Keller observed: "Whoever makes a sentence of words utters not his wisdom, but the wisdom of the race whose life is in the words, though they have never been so grouped before." And Mark Twain noted: "The difference between the right word and the almost right word is the difference between lightning and a lightning-bug." Combine the wisdom of Keller and the wit of Twain, and you can appreciate the weight of responsibility a writer can feel in deciding how to say something, anything, worth saying.)

What has been fun is the remembering. This book makes that obvious.

Some memories don't fit easily into particular categories, but merit mention, among them:

- When I told MPA Suzie Bazzani that I was writing a book about our workplace, she asked me the title. I told her. She burst into laughter, then reminded me of something she told me several years ago: When she escorts a group of students at Yorktown that I escorted earlier at Jamestown, and she introduces herself and asks them to call her Mrs. B, the students erupt in laughter and begin asking predictable questions.

- One day on the old loop, then-MPA Cindy Warner overheard me softly singing an Irish folk song, asked me to sing a little bit more, louder, then invited me to her home for a recording session. In her small recording studio, with my eyes closed I sang "Johnny, I Hardly Knew Ya" a cappella, with all of the intensity that song of rebellion inspires in me. She later mixed in a nice flute accompaniment, and put the song on a tape with the music of other local artists. Made me feel good.

- At the forge, I loved the look of genuine puzzlement on Vince Petty's face when he asked where my group was from and was answered by the teacher, Jennie Taylor, a professor of German at the College of William and Mary and one of my allies in public education activism in the community. The group, she explained, was a freshman seminar on horror films of the Weimar Republic – Nosferatu, Dr. Caligari, that sort of thing. "*What*," asked the bemused blacksmith, "does *that* have to do with Jamestown?" Said the professor: "Nothing. I just want to broaden their educational horizons." The blacksmith understood.

- "Military through the Ages" is an annual event, on the third weekend in March, bringing together dozens of re-enactment units. A guided tour on this weekend is a festival of sights and sounds and brilliant distractions. There aren't many places where one can rub elbows with Roman legionnaires and Vikings, Union and Confederate soldiers, Zulu warriors and British regulars, American and British and Russian and German units from the world wars, the National Guard of today – and, on at least one occasion when my wife and I were merely visitors, Amelia Peabody, the celebrated if fictional early 20th century English Egyptologist whose exploits my wife loves to read. Amelia was dressed perfectly for the role, and I didn't recognize her at first – Powhatan interpreter Anastasia Triantafillos. She and Dot got into a *long* conversation.

- Recently on the loop, MPA Art Edlow and I were discussing the state of the Union, sharing the same basic concerns about the dysfunction of our political system and the resulting decline in our reputation abroad, in contrast to the ideals and national self-image we were taught in school to respect. "When you and I were growing up," Art said, looking into the distance with a quiet intensity revealing his deep frustration, "we were the beacon on the hill!"

* * *

As one of the world's greatest museums, Colonial Williamsburg has long enjoyed a stellar reputation for providing extensive educational services and teacher training, and for developing talented young professionals in the field of museum operations. Most notable among the "graduates" of CW schooling are Williamsburg natives Rex Ellis, associate director of the Smithsonian's National Museum of African American History and Culture; and Christy Coleman, president of the American Civil War Center at Historic Tredegar in Richmond.

Increasingly since the early 1990s, the museums of the Jamestown-Yorktown Foundation have become widely known and well respected as teaching *and* learning institutions, strongly complementing and sometimes partnering with CW – magnificently justifying the generosity of John D. Rockefeller Jr. and vindicating the vision of the Reverend William Archer Rutherford Goodwin, the Bruton Parish rector who once declared: "I am convinced that from an historical point of view, this is the greatest teaching opportunity which exists in America." He was **so** right!

Since the establishment of the College of William and Mary in 1693, the original and continuing primary mission of the Williamsburg community has been to educate. Since 1926, Colonial Williamsburg has re-enforced this mission. Now, the Jamestown-Yorktown Foundation significantly serves the cause.

Which, by a rather roundabout way, brings me to Callie Hawkins, the most notable alumna of the J-YF School of Museum Operations.

Preparing for increased visitation approaching and during 2007, extra personnel positions were created to help handle the workload. One of the positions was filled for several years by Callie, a sweet-natured and talented young woman with a distinctive South Carolina accent and charm, which everyone appreciated – though she did say one day in the office: "My mama sent me to charm school, but she said it didn't stick."

After 2007, Callie went to work at the National Building Museum in Washington. Then she learned about a job she *really* wanted, and applied for it, telling her interviewers (in that South Carolina accent) they might as well know at the outset that her dog's name was Dixie. She got the job with the National Trust for Historic Preservation early in 2009, serving as associate director for programs at President Lincoln's Cottage in Washington and working with Ford's Theatre in teacher professional development and interpreter training. We're proud of you, Callie!

* * *

Arriving at the Settlement a few months ago to attend a State of the Foundation briefing by Phil Emerson, I encountered Phil and one of our interpreters at the back gate. As we walked, Phil jokingly said that if he got any questions he couldn't answer he hoped that we would help him out. I told him I couldn't imagine a question he couldn't handle.

I sat in the back of the crowded room. (I prefer to sit at or toward the back of a roomful of people, for two reasons. Reason 1: I see more people. Reason 2: Fewer people see me, reflecting a motto of mine: If you can't be in charge, be inconspicuous.)

Near the end of the session, Phil answered questions submitted by people in the audience. The very last question asked if the Foundation had any plans to begin offering "ghost tours" – and at the very sound of it the Spirit moved me, as it sometimes does, to speak up. "Want me to handle this one, Phil?" I called out.

Phil grinned. "Sure, Bill."

"No," I said firmly but without an exclamation point.

And that was Phil's final answer, too.

Hallelujah!

SCHEDULING

During my time as an MPA, we have been blessed by a series of three very competent and friendly schedulers – Laurie Todd, Denise Poppel and now Renee Poulsen.

The job demands competence and a friendly, cheerful spirit. Even with computer assistance, it is far from easy to match more than a hundred MPAs (with different personalities and varying days and hours of availability and occasional illnesses and car troubles and other emergencies) to thousands of diversely composed groups (with constant subtractions and additions and substitutions and changes in dates and times) at two museums 30 minutes apart.

So I do not merely nod in the direction of Renee and her predecessors; I bow.

Recently, I tried twice to reach Renee on the telephone to convey a simple message, but got her answering machine. I didn't leave my simple message either time. I waited until I reached her on the third attempt, gave her the message, then joined her in what was not possible with her answering machine, a lively, laugh-filled 10 minutes or so of friendship.

* * *

On a Saturday morning, I arrived at the Settlement on time (a half-hour early) for a tour. I waited a little more than an hour before deciding, for some reason, to check my schedule. Wrong day! The tour was the next day.

On Sunday morning, I arrived on time and waited fully 90 minutes before going home. I had spent, including travel time, about three hours of my life waiting for a group that never came. Bummer.

* * *

On a Sunday morning, I showed up for a tour with a group from Jamestown Baptist Church. I thought it odd – I had never heard of Jamestown Baptist and wondered why they were coming here instead of being in church where they belonged – but there it was on the schedule, so I went. The group never came. Very odd.

The next day, I learned that someone upstairs had been practicing with the computer scheduling system, inventing Jamestown Baptist in the process, but had neglected to delete it. Glitch.

* * *

To indicate just how confusing all of this coming and going can be, even for ordinarily well organized and sensible people, I and other MPAs have been known to show up at Jamestown for a tour clearly scheduled at Yorktown, and vice versa. It's a good idea to check one's schedule for destination and time before one goes someplace.

SECURITY

Since 1999, I've made the friendly acquaintance of dozens of G4S (formerly Wackenhut) security personnel, mostly ex-military, uniformly good people, properly professional but down-home personal. Through the years, I have developed hugging relationships with many of them.

Ray Hoyle, our security director, explained to me that the high quality of our personnel isn't accidental, that all of the people proposed for assignment at our museums must be screened to determine not only their fitness as museum security guards, but also their skills in dealing with the public; and many of the candidates don't pass Ray's muster.

One who did was the charming Puerto Rican lady who was so delightful to chat with but nobody to mess with when doing her duty. One slow day as I sat on a bench, a bus pulled into the loop, and this security guard (a former MP) began gesturing to the driver quite clearly and emphatically where to park the bus to unload. He parked the bus at the curb near me, and she went elsewhere, and then he opened the door. I said: "You're riding empty, aren't you?" He said: "Yeah, but I wasn't about to disobey that woman."

My longtime friend at Yorktown, Roy Powell, recently transferred to Hampton University. I miss him. I miss our hugs. Roy had two versions of his customary greeting when we met. In front of MPAs on the loop, it was: "Come on, Bill, let's show these MPAs some love." In front of school groups on site, it was: "Come on, Bill, let's show these children some love." And we did . . . Sometimes, I explained to puzzled students that Roy and I were brothers. They, noting the difference in our coloration, seemed more puzzled. "Hey," I said, "two ears, two eyes, one nose, one mouth, what more proof do you want?"

My current special pal is Gale Montague, a pleasant lady very popular with others on the loops at Jamestown and Yorktown.

Steve Tolbert wasn't much for hugging; a bit too dignified for that, but that's OK. He and I occasionally talked about playing a game of chess someday, but we never got around to it. I came to work one day and learned that a heart attack had claimed him. I miss him. (A bit of advice: Play the chess game! Don't wait for it to happen.)

SOCKS AND ROCKS AND COOKIES

The socks, heavy-duty winter socks made from recycled material, were a thoughtful gift from MPA

Evi Oakley, after I had substituted for her on what proved to be a miserably cold and rainy day. Great socks.

Diane Smith

The rock

As for rocks, I refer not to the type (and any old rock will do) a youngster picks up as a souvenir of his or her visit, but to the type which answers a question I've been asked several times: What's the oldest thing at the museum? Yes, it's a rock, but not just any old rock. MPA Mary Barlow, a former geology teacher, gifted me with the knowledge that there are numerous unnoticed rocks at the Settlement displaying fossilized Cambrian worm burrows approximately 500 million years old. (I picked up a small one and put it in my red bag, where it patiently waits for the next person to ask me the right question. But does that constitute theft from my employer?)

The cookies, several generous batches of them, have been gifts from MPA Cheryl Leu in thanks for providing her with transportation between Jamestown and Yorktown a couple of times. I get the best of the deal. The cookies are delicious. B wants more, which is why I'm writing this.

ABOVE AND BEYOND

It's in the little things – like really rushing to meet a last-minute need for a wheelchair from Visitor Services, or one person finding an otherwise empty new wallet with five crisp $20 bills in it and relying on others to return it to its owner (a fifth-grade girl who retrieved it within an hour), or, pre-GPS, driving from the Settlement to the York River State Park followed by a busload of Hebrew school students from New York because they sure weren't going to find it easily otherwise.

It's in simple acts of professional cooperation and courtesy, like the overcrowded day I was in the fort with a very unhappy teacher and a group of happy fourth-graders. In a subsequent memo, I lauded interpreter Brooke Pizzetti, "whom I approached at the guardhouse and (with an almost pleading tone in my voice) asked if she could give my group an interpretation, which she then did most cheerfully and skillfully, in an unhurried manner (all things considered at least a tad beyond the call of duty on such a busy day)."

Sometimes, it's a big thing. Actually, I addressed this whole subject in a memo I wrote to Anne Price-Hardister regarding Wendy Woodward, an MPA who taught from a wheelchair:

On many occasions during my more than six years with the Jamestown-Yorktown Foundation, I have been pleased, and I have felt privileged, to witness my colleagues combining great professionalism with true humanity in service to our visitors – and to our mission. It happens so often that it seems almost ordinary.

Yesterday, Wendy was extra-ordinary!

As we approached the bus loop to begin waiting for our 9:30 group, we encountered a small group of West Coast students and adults who, expecting an MPA but finding none, were preparing to go unguided, with only an hour available. So I gave them a quick orientation, and off they went . . . But Wendy wasn't satisfied. Concerned that they had come so far and had so little time to learn, she strongly suggested, and I agreed, that she would go with that group and I would take care of our group – Special Love, whose number seemed quite manageable. And Wendy drove away. (I later noted that her group had arrived many hours early, explaining the absence of an MPA.)

Special Love arrived. The number was manageable, but the circumstances were difficult. The group consisted of cancer patients and survivors, many with disabilities – really wonderful people, but presenting some logistical challenges. By the time we were nearing the end of our Indian village visit, we had a major problem – an unanticipated need for more wheelchairs, which two members of the group went to get . . . At this moment, guess who drove into the Indian village?

One good deed already done, Wendy proceeded to do another. She assumed responsibility for a small but critical number of the more severely disabled folks, thereby maximizing the opportunity for all of them to have a good experience, at their own pace.

Throughout, Wendy was as she always is, just naturally pleasant and friendly. Yesterday, to me, she shone like a bright star!

NEPOTISM!

She who got me into this situation – my wife Dot – happily joined me in it in 2004.

On her first day at work in the development office upstairs, there were welcoming flowers on her desk. From then until her last day at work in 2011, she was a great team player, one of our best, truly devoted not only to her co-workers, but also to the mission of the Jamestown-Yorktown Foundation. I am extremely proud of her service.

* * *

As a form of contribution to the Settlement, Dot (without consulting me in such a weighty financial decision) bought four bricks to be placed near the flags at the memorial plaza.

One brick was inscribed to her parents John and Eva Aldhizer, another to my parents Marvin and Nellie Bryant, another to our grandchildren Kellie, Caroline, Taylor and Abby.

The fourth was inscribed: Bill Bryant MPA Extraordinaire. It was a sweet, thoughtful thing to do, though I hoped my co-workers wouldn't see it.

WEATHER

Sometimes at the beginning of a tour, in especially good or bad weather, I'll tell my group to repeat after me: "*Every* day is a beautiful day in Virginia." Choral response. "But some days *are* more beautiful than others." Choral response.

Being a mostly outdoor museum, at Jamestown as at Yorktown, we care about the weather. A lot. For one thing, more general visitors come here when the weather is nice than when it's not. And as any MPA can testify, good weather makes a great tour possible; bad weather can ruin one. We must be prepared to teach in almost all kinds of local weather, cold or hot or just right, in rain and snow and sunshine.

Most of the time, our groups come appropriately dressed. It's fun in chilly weather to see southern California teenagers fully attired in brand-new-and-maybe-never-to-be-worn-again winter clothing. It's not fun to watch elementary school kids wet and shivering because somebody at the school didn't check the weather forecast.

As I assure my groups on days when the weatherman is unkind, B has been here long enough to know the exact location of all of the shady places, the breezy places, the sheltered places. B is not a fool, most of the time.

There is one weather condition which forces the immediate closure of the outdoor sites – thunderstorms, with lightning. It doesn't happen often, but it's a real challenge when it does, especially on busy days with hundreds of people suddenly coming inside, many to the gallery. Fortunately, the outdoor interpreters also come inside, so the teaching continues to happen. (Once, my group and I had to spend the whole two-hour tour inside the gallery. We feasted on costumed interpreters, who made it a great tour, all things considered.)

We close for hurricanes, of course.

* * *

Then there's August of 2010, when smoke from a vast fire in the Great Dismal Swamp some 50 miles from Jamestown filled the air of the Tidewater, the winds from the southwest bringing more of it to us daily.

On the 13th, I arrived at the Settlement in a fog of smoke. By the time my group and I left the village and reached the pier – from which you could not see the island – I had decided that my kids shouldn't be breathing this stuff (and neither should I). I was sure the teacher would agree. By then, however, the decision had been made to evacuate the outdoor sites, which we were happy to do, promptly. It was awful out there.

In retrospect, the group (and I) should never have gone outside.

* * *

On a cold, cold winter day, with snow thick on the ground and a brisk wind constantly blowing, I had already survived two outside tours for Visitor Services and was waiting indoors to see if anybody dared to show up for the 3:30 tour, praying nobody would, envisioning the welcoming fire in the fireplace at home.

At 3:25, the wind suddenly increased and the snow returned with blizzard intensity. And two people eagerly showed up – from Germany. Then came a group of three – from Switzerland. Then came an older couple, who reported that when they got on the plane that morning in Butte, Montana, the temperature was -40!

To their great credit, all of them assured me that the tour wasn't necessary, that they would fully understand if I preferred not to go. But I said: "No, you folks have come a long way . . . . . Let's go!"

As thoroughly miserable as that tour was weather-wise, at least for me, we managed to have a lot of fun.

The fire in the fireplace at home was never more appreciated.

* * *

On a hot, hot day during the busy summer of 2007, I had already done two tours for Visitor Services and was very, very, very tired when I drove back to the Settlement, found a space and parked.

Slowly I opened the door, and slowly I placed my left foot on the ground, and . . . I froze, utterly unwilling and/or unable to move.

That's when I spoke to myself, out loud: "You can do this . . . . . You gotta do this . . . . . Do this!"

I did it!

I have often thought of that day, and have recalled it occasionally while writing this book . . . You can do this. You gotta do this. Do this!

Sometimes it is helpful to remember the past, to inspire the present.

* * *

There's nothing you can do about the weather – except to dress for it or move to where it's better – and that's probably a good thing. Whoever *can* influence or control the weather has a huge responsibility. The Good Lord once forgot to turn off the rain for 40 days, and look what happened.

In threatening weather, I sometimes ask my groups at the beginning of a tour to repeat after me: No rain! "No rain!" No rain!! "No rain!!" No rain!!! "No rain!!!" Hey, it worked at Woodstock, although I do add: Please. "Please." Always helps to ask nicely.

One day, after the students had reassembled from a preliminary visit to the restrooms, I did this no-rain routine with a Catholic school group. A parent advised me that if I wanted to get a message through to God I should talk to an elderly woman sitting on a bench nearby "because she's closer to God than anybody else here." So I went over to the woman, who seemed happy to see me, and preparatory to asking her intervention I leaned over and planted a light kiss on the top of her head – and she exclaimed in unbridled joy: "That's the first time I've been kissed in 50 years! Quick! Somebody take a picture!

Quick!" Several people took several pictures as I repeated the gesture twice.

She did not come with us on the tour. In the village, I learned that the school was established some years ago by a maverick nun very unhappy with the conventional curriculum. So you know whom I had kissed. (And it did not rain.)

* * *

On a cool but not cold (at least to me) morning in March, a group of students from Bermuda arrived. All they wanted to talk about was snow, whether we'd be seeing any, when, what it would be like. Several times during the tour, I reminded them that the temperature was 42 degrees and that it didn't snow at 42. I hated to disappoint them, repeatedly, but facts are facts, right?

Wrong. That afternoon, with the temperature still at 42 and the youngsters from Bermuda touring Colonial Williamsburg, it began to snow – huge, fluffy flakes, the biggest flakes of snow I've ever seen – and I knew, for a fact that those kids were joyfully joking among themselves: That old man didn't know what he was talking about!

CRITTERS

Naturally, we've got all kinds of critters (fortunately no longer including the saber-toothed tigers and mastodons which once roamed this land so many years or so ago).

Understandably, one rarely sees the worms and seldom notices the ants which inhabit this place. (Reportedly, about 80 percent of Earth's biomass lives under the ground. Just to keep things in perspective, there's a mostly underground mushroom in Oregon which at 2,200 acres is larger than Jamestown Island, which at 1,500 acres is three times the size of the city-state of Monaco, which with a population of 37,579 more or less is the smallest and most densely inhabited member of the United Nations!)

Above ground: Squirrels, snakes, lizards, turtles, rabbits, possums, raccoons, muskrats, an occasional deer. One day, waiting at the loop, two other MPAs and I watched not one, not two but three red foxes on the prowl across the Jamestown Road – the first foxes any of us had seen in this region.

Well above ground much of the time: Flying critters. Lots of 'em. The smallest you can barely see, seasonal swarms of them pestering almost everyone at varying places on site; and it's difficult to teach when many of your students (and adults) are flailing their arms in the air in defense against the invasion, when, in fact, resistance is futile. Then there are the flies, moths, wasps, butterflies, bees – and, of course, the birds.

The most conspicuous at Jamestown are the chickens, which roam inside and around the fort, occasionally wandering over to the village to dine on corn clumsily pounded out of the corn grinders by modern youngsters not educated in the old ways. At Yorktown, the fowl population includes chickens, turkeys, guinea hens and Muscovy ducks.

We have the usual backyard birds – robins, doves, crows, owls, hawks, finches and such. Plus, and this is a real plus, we have the birds who like to live near the river (with its abundant supply of many kinds of fish) – gulls, herons, egrets, ospreys . . . and eagles!

Some years ago, the bald eagle was a very endangered species in Virginia and extinct along the James River, but Mitchell Byrd and other good people made a great effort to protect and preserve it. Now, there are approximately 1,400 nesting eagle sites in Virginia, many along the James – including, for the past couple of years, a very large nest at the top of a tall pine tree in the village. This spring of 2014, our eagles begat a fledgling, adding to the daily drama of the village, to the delight of thousands of visitors. (During this same time, ospreys have built an even larger nest atop the Discovery Tower. Sometimes, according to our people in the village, the neighborhood ospreys and eagles squabble, rather noisily.)

One day several years ago in the village, an eagle settled onto a tree limb, not very high up, and dined on a fish the whole time my group was there. Great sideshow!

On a busy day at the pier, a parent with my group tugged my sleeve and asked: "B, what does an eagle look like?" Without looking up, I said: "Don't worry. When you see one, you'll know it." Then she said: "Is that one?" I looked up – and there it was, circling about 10 feet above the end of the pier – and then it was joined by its mate and they circled together – and then together they flew the whole distance of the pier at that low level. Super sideshow!!

Diane Smith

A chicken

On at least two occasions, fish have visited the Settlement, dropped from the sky by birds. One fish landed in the village, another in the fort. Both were properly cooked and consumed.

Occasionally, on the pier, I casually ask my groups not to wake up the alligator. You'd be surprised how many students (and adults) begin looking for the alligator. Silly people.

* * *

As a rule, I do not compete with certain critters.

When my students are distracted by chickens or roosters, it's easy and usually advisable to regain the group's attention, though I do it slowly when the kids are from the inner city or urban areas where chickens are rarely if ever sighted. (Besides, they're actually very pretty chickens and roosters, especially the latter. I didn't fully appreciate such birds until I encountered the ones at Jamestown and Yorktown.)

Likewise, it's not difficult to keep a group focused in the presence of the occasional curious bee or the wandering wee spider probably more afraid of us than we should be of it.

But when my people are distracted by an eagle posing majestically on a tree branch or soaring mightily overhead, or by a snake lazily sunning itself on the rocks at the pier, or by a little muskrat busily swimming along . . . I do not compete. I join in the fun of watching. After all, *this* is what my people will be remembering at day's end. Why shouldn't *I* also have the pleasure of remembering it?)

* * *

I should make some reference to the unseen birds, dog and cat which inhabit the gallery and enliven the experience, surprising some people with their unexpected sudden singing, barking and meowing in a few appropriate places.

The birds (plural because they change indoors according to the season outdoors) are a problem, to me. As I occasionally say to a group when a bird begins to sing *so sweetly*: "That bird is getting on my nerves! Every time I start to say something important, that bird starts singing. Now, I like listening to birds, and every time that bird starts to sing I start to listen – So if I get distracted, you don't blame *me*! You blame . . ."

"The *bird*!!!"

* * *

I love telling this story to my groups.

One quiet summer day at Yorktown, very early in my experience there, I was sitting on a bench near the walkway leading to the exit, doing visitor surveys, waiting for some folks to come along who might be willing to spend a few minutes answering some questions about their experience. All was peaceful.

Then, shockingly, Tom the turkey introduced himself, very loudly, directly behind where I was sitting. He got my attention! So I did the civilized thing and replied, in what I had always thought was a pretty good turkey imitation.

Tom answered. I answered him. We carried on a nice conversation.

Subsequently, on tours there, when encountering Tom at the farm, either he or I would start a brief conversation, much to the delight of my school groups, especially the younger kids.

Then, one day, Tom wasn't in a mood to talk, so I led my group of fifth-graders away from him, toward the tobacco barn. As we walked, a boy said: "B, would you like to hear a turkey?" I said: "Sure." He then proceeded to speak *perfect* turkey! If you had closed your eyes, you would have sworn he was a turkey. I was amazed, as was the whole group, so I turned to the boy's father and asked: "Where did he learn **that**!" To which the father replied: "He was raised on a turkey farm."

Of course!

That's not the end of the story. The next day, I was at Jamestown, finishing a tour with some fifth-graders, and as we walked I told the turkey story to a father, who was amused. Then his daughter – a wisp of a little girl – asked, in a very soft voice: "B, would you like to hear a horse?" Hesitating slightly at the thought of it, I said: "Uh, sure." Well, that girl began prancing around speaking *perfect* horse! If you had closed your eyes, you would have sworn there was a half-ton steed neighing nearby. I was speechless as I turned to the father. "She was raised," he said with a smile, "on a horse farm."

Of course!

When I tell this story to my groups, I add: "Just think about what your fine minds can learn if you really try. If you apply yourselves, *you* might someday be able to speak perfect turkey or perfect horse!

History does not pose problems without eventually producing solutions. The disenchanted, the disadvantaged and the disinherited seem, at times of deep crisis, to summon up some sort of genius that enables them to perceive and capture the appropriate weapons to carve out their destiny.
Martin Luther King Jr.

CHAPTER 5: TOOLS

A DEFINITION

A tool is a thing, tangible or otherwise, useful in doing a job. The number and variety of tools of the trade available to a teacher are limited only by the teacher's resources and imagination.

In the right circumstances, a simple smile can be an effective tool; likewise, a mild frown. Humor is a great tool.

My attitude is: If it helps to get and keep their attention, use it. If it helps to enliven the experience and enhance the possibility of learning, use it. If it helps to illustrate or demonstrate a lesson, use it. If it helps to solve a mystery or makes a point crystal clear, use it. If it simply makes people laugh, use it.

Even if it's "unconventional" or rather odd or maybe even very goofy, if it gits 'er done, use it! My ponytail has been a tool of sorts – not to mention my wounded index finger, and, most notably, I suppose, my nose.

Rewards are tools of approval and encouragement. But instead of mere praise or an A-plus, I prefer a high-five or a fist-bump – or on special occasions, when a youngster's answer or thought is particularly excellent, a double fist-bump with fingery fireworks and appropriate sound effects.

I suppose my teaching "persona" is a combination of late Abraham Lincoln and early Robin Williams. (Can you believe how that guy's acting career morphed him from Mork of Ork into Dwight Eisenhower? Nanu nanu, Ike!)

* * *

Every MPA is equipped with a different shoulder bag for each museum, each bag providing not only space for a clipboard (with necessary paperwork and helpful historical information and visual aides), but also pouches for a wide variety of replica artifacts.

The red bag at Jamestown includes, among other things, a Powhatan bone needle and sinew thread, English scissors, a shafted arrowhead, a sea biscuit, a chunk of fool's gold (a quantity of which the first colonists optimistically sent back to England for analysis) and a ship's whistle.

The blue bag at Yorktown includes, among other things, colonial banknotes and coins, a packaged deck of playing cards as it would have appeared on Stamp Act paper, a parchment copy of the Declaration of Independence, a musket ball made of lead and a pencil made from a musket ball and dice made from musket balls, which were thus very useful not only for hurting the enemy, but also for writing to the folks back home and getting in trouble for gambling in camp.

Some examples of other "tools" I employ:

Sound

One day, I was down below on the Susan squatting with a seated group, knowing (as I had forewarned them) that soon we would hear the big cannon in the fort being fired, so be prepared; but we weren't prepared for the boom which came, shocking all of us and making us jump up a bit.

Imagine battle.

* * *

More than once, to encourage a group including students of Latin, I have launched into the opening of Cicero's First Catalinarian Oration, just enough to let them sense the emotion and drama of those dead words at the moment they were originally spoken.

Maybe it's showboating, but it seems to have a good effect on the students, and the teachers seem to approve.

* * *

Toward the end of a tour with fifth-graders, I noticed a girl by herself near the blacksmith shop, just looking around. I don't think she had said a word the whole tour, to anybody; instead of listening, she just looked around. She seemed interested, but not engaged. I asked a teacher: "What's her story?"

The teacher explained that the girl had just arrived from Russia and didn't speak any English.

So I strolled over to her and wished her a good day and asked how she was doing, and with a beautiful smile of discovery she shyly said she was doing well, thank you very much, and asked how I was doing, and I said I was doing great, and that was enough to seal the deal . . . Made her day, I suspect. Made mine, I know.

Locations

At the start of a tour, to introduce the Jamestown experience and myself, occasionally I lead a group toward a shady place near the Discovery Tower, then herd them "into the house" – actually, the approximate archaeological footprint of a farmhouse which was there in 1640, fronting on the Great Road out of Jamestown.

When the people who lived in that house went to sleep at night, what was on their minds?

* * *

At the end of a tour in the fort, often I stop a group near the back gate, then select a girl or woman and guide her to a specific place, facing the group – standing where Queen Elizabeth stood when she spoke here in 2007.

Having thus briefly crowned a queen (who often knows how the real one customarily waves her hand), I let the group know that I have greatly admired Elizabeth the person since before she became Elizabeth the queen, but I also let them know B's little-d democratic attitude: If I can't be king, **nobody** can!

Nails

A nail is a tool. And I'm not talkin' about your simple ordinary run-of-the-mill circular nail with a pointed end that invisibly splits the wood into which it's driven. No, I'm talkin' about a genuine hand-forged nail with a square shaft tapering to a pointed end, the kind that distributes the pressure and doesn't split the wood.

Whenever I approach the blacksmith shop, I scan the discarded coal ashes on the ground for rusted rejects exposed to the surface by recent rain. Sometimes, I put one in my bag. Sometimes, I use it on the spot. So which is the better nail? And why don't we make nails that way today?

National Geographic

When the National Geographic published a major story about Jamestown, I carried a copy of the magazine in my bag.

On the pier, I opened it to a particular two-page photo of the Susan Constant with interpreter Kristen Detwiler staring toward an imagined sea, showing it to the group standing where the photographer stood, sometimes pointing to Kristen herself nearby.

The magazine became so worn and torn from being pulled out of and stuffed into my bag that I had to discontinue using it.

Cellphones

In the church, I ask if anyone has a cell phone I might have, preferably one with Internet service. There's always one. I accept it, put it in my pocket and thank the former owner, saying I've always wanted one of these, which causes puzzlement. (A girl asked to have hers back for just a minute. I asked why. "To call the police," she said.)

Outside the church, I explain: Forty years or so ago, the biggest computer in the world was up at MIT, the Massachusetts Institute of Technology. It weighed about 18 tons. It cost about $12 million. And everybody at the university had to share the one computer. You had to reserve time on it.

That was then. Now, the computer chip controlling this device – the cell phone – costs, on average, about $12. That's a millionth the cost of the MIT computer. It's a millionth the size of the MIT computer. It's a million times **more powerful** than the MIT computer. "And," I conclude, returning the phone to its proper owner, "it's all yours . . . *Imagine* the power in your hands, compared to only 40 years ago." Then to the group: "And you ain't seen nothin' yet! Your grandchildren are gonna ask you: Grandma, grandpa, you mean they didn't have holographic television when you were a child?"

Live Long and Prosper

As my older students assemble for our final chat, I raise my hand in the Vulcan manner. There are usually several wannabe Vulcans in the crowd.

I solemnly summon a student forward, note that this is the only place in Virginia where you can get a Vulcan high-five, then offer my hand. If the student somehow finds the situation to be humorous, I rebuke him or her. "Get rid of that silly smile," I say. "We Vulcans don't show emotions." Few succeed, and I just nod at them. The others I scornfully dismiss as part Klingon, then turn my Vulcan gesture into a fist and pump the air with it and shout: "Qapla!" Success! Occasionally, a wannabe Klingon replies. Usually, numerous Vulcan high-fives ensue.

Recently, with a quiet and reserved yet seemingly pleasant man accompanying his daughter's class, I had a chance to ask what he did in real life. He said he was a lawyer. I asked where he went to law school. Harvard, he replied. I offered my compliments, sincerely, because I have heard that Harvard has a very good law school . . . At the end of the tour, only he, now smiling slightly, held up his hand in the Vulcan manner. I somberly told him to step forward, then began the high-five – but as hard as he tried he could not contain his amusement with this unexpected odd scene in front of the class, so I dismissed him as Klingon, then informed the group: "The Klingons send their best students to Harvard." The lawyer laughed.

Sometimes, with a straggler wanting to shake my hand, I offer instead to teach him or her the Secret Bryant-Varble Handshake (a seven-phase process created with my close friend Mike Varble), now being used all across the nation and around the world. Other stragglers, seeing this, want me to teach them, too, so I do.

* * *

Which brings us to "Duck Dynasty," the TV show featuring the Robertson family and their friends in Louisiana, and to the following letter to Willie Robertson:

Willie . . .

I'm a teacher at the Jamestown Settlement living history museum in Williamsburg, Virginia, providing instructional tours to groups from all over the world, particularly school groups from throughout the United States. To enhance my teaching, I naturally try to bond with each of my groups early on, doing or saying something to get their close attention, often with humor.

Recently, with groups of middle school and high school students from California, Washington, Utah, Minnesota, Illinois, Pennsylvania and two boroughs of New York City, I have pointedly asked each group, very early on, to make me "happy, happy, happy" – to which most of the kids and many of the adults in all groups have responded with surprise, delight and laughter, a testament to the widespread popularity and wholesome fun of your family's show. (With each of my groups, there has been some difference of opinion as to whether I more closely resemble Phil or Si. I am not sure what to make of this confusion.)

Just thought you'd be interested in this additional insight into the "Duck Dynasty" experience.

Keep it real, more or less, and keep it wholesome.

If any of y'all ever have occasion to be in this vicinity, I'd be very pleased to help provide some Virginia hospitality.

Cordial regards to all of your family.

Sincerely . . . Bill Bryant

Postscript: Twice since sending that letter, I have directly asked out-of-state groups if I more closely resemble Phil or Si. With both, the answer was unanimous: Si! And that's a fact, Jack!

* * *

For several years, inspired by the TV cartoon "Powerpuff Girls" watched religiously by my grandchildren and me, I kept in my bag and frequently used a formidable disciplinary weapon, a laminated picture of the show's archvillain, a monkey-like character who spoke in a deep gravelly voice hard to mimic.

With elementary school kids, I warned them that if they didn't behave well, I would reach into my bag and (reaching into my bag) bring forth: "**Mojo Jojo!** There can be only one Mojo Jojo! Only one Mojo Jojo can there be!"

Kids liked the Powerpuff Girls.

They loved Mojo Jojo.

He is still in my bag. I'm not sure why. Maybe it's because someday, someone of just the right age will remember him, and he can be a tool again.

Bulletin: The Powerpuff Girls – and Mojo Jojo – have returned to Nickelodeon in reruns, as I learned recently with a group of fourth-graders who were thrilled when I mentioned the show, then reached deep into my bag and brought forth – *Mojo Jojo!!!*

HALLELUJAH!

It started one morning a few years ago down below on the Susan. Preparing to describe the foul conditions on the 'tween deck in 1607, I routinely asked my group to take a deep breath, and hold it . . . and release it . . . and, I impulsively added, say *Hallelujah!*

"Hallelujah!" they responded so quickly and naturally that I asked them to say it again, which more loudly they did. *"Hallelujah!!"* One more time, young brothers and sisters. *"Hallelujah!!!"*

"If you had taken that same deep breath on board the original Susan Constant in 1607," I said, "you couldn't have handled it. You'd have keeled over from the stench." Then I described the foul conditions down below – which on the Susan included the aroma of chickens, pigs, goats and dogs in the heavy cargo deck – noting that it didn't smell a whole lot better back in England or anywhere else on the planet at the time, and told

213

them to be thankful for the air they breathe today. At the end, I asked them to take another deep breath, and hold it . . . and release it . . . "And what do you say?"

"Hallelujah!!!"

I suggested that they say it again when they got back on the bus for the comfortable ride home.

* * *

Since then, my *Hallelujah* choruses have been heard at various places, celebrating not only particular advantages and blessings we enjoy today because of the struggle and sacrifice of earlier people, but also numerous specific instances where the very survival of the colony was aided by great good luck or Providence, such as:

What if they had hung the trouble-maker John Smith before he could even get to Jamestown?

What if the chief of the Pasbeheghs had succeeded in drowning Smith in their personal combat near our pier?

What if the colonists who *abandoned* Jamestown following the Starving Time hadn't encountered the first of the incoming relief ships?

What if any one of the three fleets sent by the King of Spain to attack and destroy Jamestown had arrived instead of being dispersed by hurricanes and a mutiny?

What if Chanco hadn't bravely warned the settlers on the island about the impending assault along the James?

What if the Powhatans had learned in the turmoil following the 1622 assault that the English had run out of gunpowder?

Where would we be today if any of these "ifs" had happened?

They didn't!

Hallelujah!!!

* * *

One day in the church, I asked a middle school group to say *Hallelujah*. And there was puzzled silence. "B," a teacher said, "we are a Catholic school. May we say *huzzah* instead?"

Wondering what being a Catholic school had to do with it, I said: "Sure."

"Huzzah! . . . Huzzah!! . . . Huzzah!!!"

Whatever works for you.

* * *

I confess and/or profess: I do sometimes refer to my teaching philosophy as the Hallelujah School of History, and I do sometimes display a certain passion, an evangelical fervor, which sometimes surprises even me.

The people of the past **and** the people of the present **and** the people of the future inspire (and in a sense command) me, in a way I cannot adequately explain.

FLEXADAPTABILITY

The most important word in MPA training, theory and practice is "flexibility" (which I combine with "adaptability" to complete the meaning) – not only as a complex of methodology, for dealing with the unusual and unexpected, but also as a governing attitude, a preparedness and willingness to depart from the routine, whether because of dire sudden necessity or a deliberate decision to pursue an alternative, better path to learning.

I think of it as "independence of command," and like most MPAs I exercise it on almost every tour. On a busy day, even an intimately familiar site can be like uncharted territory, MPAs leading their groups in hopeful search of finding an available interpreter or yehakin or ship or activity site, somewhere. (This is one of the reasons I instruct my groups to stay behind me, because, as I occasionally explain to them while I'm looking desperately around, sometimes I really don't know where I'm going.)

I was waiting with other MPAs on the loop at Yorktown one day when two busloads of teenagers arrived early, before some of their guides had arrived. I left the loop long enough to help unload the buses and herd the students to a gathering place, then, at the request of one of their guides, started to speak to them, buying time but trying not to kill it. I spoke for upwards of 15 minutes, until the other guides finally arrived (on time), then scurried back to the loop just as my own people arrived.

Flexadaptibility!

MEDICAL MATTERS

I have experienced no serious medical emergencies on my tours, with the possible exception of the time Kristen Detwiler encountered me in the fort and easily persuaded me to go home, saying she would take the group the rest of the way. A few days later, a doctor I was visiting for another reason told me I had probably suffered a mild heat stroke. (The next year, in the fort, the teacher with that group spotted me, came over and said she was so glad to see me again, that she had been worrying all year.)

At Jamestown, a boy had a nosebleed in the village. I didn't go to medical school, but I did have nosebleeds when I was a kid and knew what to do. The boy did what I told him to do. Cured!

In the encampment at Yorktown, a girl had an epileptic seizure. I managed to cradle the back of her head as she (and I) slumped to the ground. The school nurse stepped forward and took charge. Within minutes, the girl was back to normal.

* * *

I'll mention sneezes and hiccups not because they really fit into this category, but because I can't think of a more appropriate category and I'm sure not going to create a new one just for them. So . . .

There's nothing lonelier than an unblessed sneeze – or, as I like to say, an ungesundheited achoo – so I tend to react instinctively when I hear one, such as: "How many rivers gesundheit flow into the Chesapeake Bay?" . . . With a group of Mexican high school girls one day, a girl sneezed. "Gesundheit," I said as all of her classmates said: "Salud." A minute later, the girl sneezed again. "Salud," I said as all of her classmates said: "Gesundheit." Cultures in contact!

I have fun with hiccups, telling an afflicted student not to worry, that if it continues I have the cure – a painful cure, it's true, but sure to do the job. Only once in about a hundred cases has the mere threat of this cure failed to solve the problem. Then, yes, I did apply the cure. I can't describe it adequately. All you need to know is that it involves a healthy dose of laughter and does not require tickling, which would be inappropriate touching.

* * *

Mental health is very important. Every now and then, some of us need an attitude adjustment, administered by someone who cares.

More than five months since giving my last tour at Yorktown (five months of dramatic changes there), I arrived recently in a subdued and somewhat apprehensive mood, welcomed by MPAs Joni Carlson and Rich Watkins. Joni asked me how I was doing, and I said: "So far, so good." She said that wasn't good enough, that I needed some motivation, then offered me our customary hug. While Joni and I hugged, Rich cracked: "A hug, a kick in the butt. Whatever it takes."

Several days in a row as I led my groups onto the Susan, Kristen (she who rescued me that hot day in the fort) had greeted me at the top of the gangway and cheerfully asked how I was doing, and I had replied in a less than happy manner, grumbling about something or other. Finally, she had enough of it and sternly told me so, and told me to cheer up. I thought about it, and the next time I met her at the top of the gangway I greeted her cheerfully and declared: "It may be true that you can't teach an old dog new tricks, but you sure can tell him to shut up! Thank you!" Back to normal.

In RETIREMENT

Especially at Jamestown, the content of my tour has changed significantly since I began constructing it in 1999 – not so much the core historical material as the ways I teach it. It is a work in progress even now.

Sometimes, to accommodate new information and insights and methods, I have ceased using really good routines. In at least three instances, I really regret it, and deep down am determined to revive them someday.

Wingapo (Hello)

At the entrance to the Powhatan section in the old gallery, I would stop my group and ask a boy or girl to stand in front me. Then it went something like this:

"I am a Powhatan, and you are an Englishman. We are making first contact. I am wearing only a deerskin cloth around my hips. My clean-shaven face is painted red and black. My head is shaved bald on one side, with a ponytail on the other and an eagle's feather sticking in it, and one of my pierced ears has a hawk's claw in it (or perhaps a knotted hissing snake). I am covered with bear grease.

"You are dressed from head to toe – shoes, socks, pants, shirt, some sort of hard shiny thing on your chest, another strange-looking object on your head. Your skin is pale, your face mostly covered by hair. I say to you: Wingapo." At this point, I would also say a few brief sentences in fake Algonquian, ending with an unintelligible question, then: "And you say? . . . (laughter) . . . Do we have a problem here?" Then I would talk briefly about the obvious differences and not so obvious human similarities of the two cultures.

Once (and only once), instead of fake Algonquian, I decided to speak Italian with a fifth-grade girl. "Buon giorno, ragazza. Come' stai?" To which she replied: "Bene, grazie, signore. E come' sta Lei oggi?" What are the odds?!

"All men . . . "

In the vestibule of the old gallery, preparing to take my people outside, I would sit them down on the benches and invite an adult (a man) to stand next to me.

"I am the richest man in England in 1607. This man has little or nothing. Is this man equal to me?" No, of course not.

"Now I am Bill Gates. This guy still has little or nothing. Is this man my equal?" Yes, of course. The man and I then shook hands. The students got the point. So do you.

Getting into the role-playing spirit, a woman once interrupted me to ask, to the delight of the group: "B, can I be *Mrs.* Bill Gates?"

Footnote: This is in the if-you're-looking-for-signs-of-progress-you-can-find-them category. More than a decade ago, with a group from an all-white private academy in the Delta of Mississippi, I learned from the principal (who also happened to be chairman of the local public school board) that he was recruiting black students to attend the academy. So when I did this routine in the vestibule and the time came to shake hands, we shook hands in the conventional manner as I began chatting with him about his visit and shifted from the conventional handshake into the second phase of a more elaborate handshake, and our thumbs locked, he was with me, so I shifted into the third phase, and our fingers clinched, he was with me, so I shifted toward an up-and-down fist bump – and he hesitated, then nudged against my arm with his elbow, saying with a warm smile in a rich Delta accent: "That's how we're learnin' to do it down in Mississippi!" A wonderful, revealing moment.

Footnote to the footnote: My brother-in-law Loeb is from the Delta. Roomed with Trent Lott at the university. Visiting from Minnesota a few years ago, Loeb and my sister Janice had dinner with me and my wife Dot and a very special guest, Bruce Turner, descendant of Nat. It was a joy watching Loeb and Bruce become good friends quickly (even before each became aware of the other's experience with computers and advanced technology), but not a surprise. Both men are disposed to be friendly and easy to befriend; if you don't like *them*, there's something wrong with *you*. That dinner scene, with its generous servings of comradeship and laughter, remains a beautiful memory.

A Mere Penny

On the pier at the map showing the route of the first voyage to Jamestown, I developed the "lucky (or magic) penny" routine.

I would stop my group, note that the initial voyage took 144 days, then ask: "Nowadays, if you wanted to go from London to Virginia, how would you probably do it?" By airplane, probably a jet.

"What was the fastest commercial jet ever in service?" Usually, someone in the group knows about the Concorde.

"On a Concorde jet, between this time today and this time tomorrow, in the space of 24 hours, you," I said, turning around and bracing myself, "can go from here (pounding London) to here (pounding Jamestown) to here (pound) to here (pound) to here (pound) to here (pound) to here (pound) to here (pound) to here (really hard pound)," I'd say, turning around to face them, "in **one** day! Which means that in the time it took *them* to cross the Atlantic once, in great danger and discomfort, not knowing if they would get here, *you* today can cross the Atlantic more than a thousand times, eating first-class food, watching a movie, reading a book, sleeping, in virtually perfect safety. And that's *at least* the difference between a $10 bill and a penny.

"Which would you rather have?" The $10 bill! "And your pockets are *stuffed* with $10 bills compared to people back then, who had only pennies. And I'm not just talking about how fast we can go from one place to another. In commerce, religion, politics, industry, medicine and countless other fields of human endeavour, we're a thousand times or more better off than they were."

Then I would hold up a penny and ask who wanted it. I'd pick a student (or an adult in an adults-only group), then with proper ceremony present the penny, saying it would bring him or her good luck if he or she kept it, making the recipient promise, whenever looking at the penny – or any other penny – to think about the advantages we enjoy today, and to think about Mr. Lincoln.

* * *

With a group of fifth-graders, when I asked which would you rather have, a $10 bill or a penny, a boy firmly answered: "A penny."

He seemed very sure of himself, so I asked: "Which one?"

"This one," he said, reaching into his pocket and producing a coin sleeve containing a 1909 Lincoln S-VDB (San Francisco mint with the initials of designer Victor D. Brenner). I fondled it.

"How much you want for it?"

"Not for sale," he said, repocketing the gem.

Too bad. I always wanted one of those.

Footnote: On the Internet, I recently saw a perfectly detailed photograph of a Philadelphia-minted 1909 Lincoln penny showing dust on it. The penny is on Mars! The photo was taken by the amazing rover Curiosity. Who at NASA had the genius to send Mr. Lincoln to Mars?! I googled the answer: Ken Edgett. Huzzah, Ken!!!

NASA

**Mr. Lincoln lightly touched by
the red dust of Mars**

＊ ＊ ＊

One day, while I was making this presentation, a girl passing nearby with her family called out to me: "B! Do you remember me?" I said she did look a little familiar (though she didn't). She said: "I was here with my school group last year from California, and you gave me one of your magic pennies. I just want you to know, B," she continued, pulling out of her purse a small plastic baggie with a penny in it, "my year has been *fan*tastic!"

In 2008, Visitor Services passed along a note to me: "B . . . Our names are Shari & Rodney and one year ago on your tour we were the lucky recipients of your 'lucky penny.' Just wanted to thank you and let you know we are now married as of 8-8-08. Thanks for the penny. Much love . . . Rodney & Shari Estes."

By golly, maybe the things *are* lucky.

TRAFFIC

"Traffic management," I sometimes remark to a nearby adult as I navigate my group through a crowded site, "is a big part of this job."

Site awareness must be constant. MPA cooperation and courtesy are essential. Otherwise, the system wouldn't work.

Happily, almost all MPAs demonstrate common sense in heavy traffic almost all of the time. There are exceptions, of course, usually by new and inexperienced MPAs but sometimes by veterans. On several occasions, albeit inadvertently, I myself have been guilty of lapses in judgment. (In the office following tours, it's not uncommon to hear an MPA apologizing for blocking or cutting off another's group, the apology sometimes mutual and always accepted. Very professional, and polite.)

What can happen when the rules of the road are ignored? Some examples:

- In the fort, three groups led by veteran MPAs converged approaching the back entrance. We slowed down, establishing eye contact, beginning a silent communication to avoid a logjam – when a fourth group led by a new MPA came barreling right through the narrow gap available. There was no collision, but the mindlessness was blatant.

- With a large group aboard the small Discovery, the interpreter and I stood with our backs to the pier. Suddenly, there was a commotion behind us. By the time I turned around, a fine MPA (who really should have known better) was leading his large group onto the ship. It was too late to stop them, so I immediately interrupted the interpreter and began quickly evacuating my people. Not a good scene.

- In the gallery at Yorktown, I was being closely pursued by Don Swain's group (with another group not far behind him) when I had to stop because a new MPA had parked her group at the base of the rampway, sitting down. After a few minutes, it seemed like the group was moving out, so I moved my group forward – and stopped, because the MPA had sat 'em down again further up the ramp! All I could do was look at Don and shrug, a silent message he passed along to the MPA now parked behind him.

- In the old gallery at Jamestown, the popular light display illustrating early settlement was in a bad location. A group stopping there blocked the main hallway, requiring another group to worm through a narrow adjacent exhibit area. On busy days, not unreasonably, stopping at the lights was an absolute no-no. Still, it was hard to resist the lights, a great teaching tool enjoyed by youngsters and oldsters alike. Some MPAs couldn't resist when a reasonable opportunity presented itself. One day, two of my supervisors decided to accompany me for part of the tour. I brought my group to the lights, checked the traffic situation, stopped, and said: "I'm not supposed to stop here on a busy day. If my supervisors learn about this, I could be in some real trouble. So you have to promise me you won't tell my supervisors." They promised, and the show was on. Later, my supervisors said not a word about it. They were former MPAs. They understood.

HANDS (ET CETERA) ON

As "living history" museums, we place much emphasis on the "hands-on" experience, especially for younger people. Accordingly, there's a lot of cordage-making, knot-tying (and untying), rope-pulling, barrel-lifting, biscuit-feeling – literally hands-on activity.

But I feel, as do most MPAs, that this definition is much too narrow in describing the physically engaging experience of living history. Consider:

- The butt-on experience . . . sitting on a deerskin-covered bed in a Powhatan yehakin, on a cramped low bench or the bare floor down below on the Susan, on the hard pews in the church.

- The eyes-on experience . . . seeing the gallery exhibits, the realistic village and ships and fort, plus the very real and beautiful river, and the interpreters in their curious costumes. Commonly, I hear expressions of wonderment behind me as we enter the gallery or approach an outdoor site, especially at first sight of the ships. ("I am not imagining this!" I recently heard a girl exclaim as we entered the village.)

- The ears-on experience . . . hearing the firing of the musket (and sometimes a ship's gun), the piping of the ship's whistle, the engaging voices and stories of the interpreters.

- The nose-on experience . . . smelling the cookfire in the village, the sweet honeysuckle down near the pier, the strangely pleasing scent of spent gunpowder, the stew being cooked in the fort kitchen.

- Alas, I cannot think of an activity involving the sense of taste. The closest we come is the mere sight and smell of food cooking. Unfortunately (or fortunately), we cannot let our visitors eat what we cook because the Virginia Department of Health says we have unsanitary kitchens! However, as a state employee I can taste it, and do attest that the Powhatan cornbread is quite tasty when laced with berries and nuts, that Gretchen Johnson's freshly baked apple pie at Yorktown is wonderful, and that one type of English bread at Jamestown is the most delicious B has ever tasted! (I would pay $20 for a loaf of that bread. I really would.)

As friend Diane Smith observed on my evaluation after a recent visit: "The ability to see & hear & touch is invaluable."

*It is a part of the American character
to consider nothing as desperate –
to surmount every difficulty
by resolution and contrivance.*
Thomas Jefferson

CHAPTER 6: PEOPLE ON TOUR

NOTABLE

Most of the people who visit our museums are ordinary folks. Some are well known, or otherwise important in some way. Notable visitors I've personally encountered include:

- A descendant of King Kamehameha of Hawaii, whom I mention not because the descendant himself is famous but because he represents dozens of visitors and co-workers descended from significant historical characters, not to mention the scores of Pocahontas progeny. (One day in the gallery at Yorktown, approaching the Lafayette exhibit with a group including several families from Annapolis, Maryland, a boy shyly noted that he was a descendant of Lafayette, so I mentioned this to the group. A man leaned forward and modestly said: "Actually, quite a few of us are." I called for a show of hands. I don't recall the exact number, but *most* of them were descendants, still living in the area where some of Lafayette's descendants chose to live.)

- Colonel Gail Halvorsen, the Candyman of the Berlin Airlift, whose payloads during that 1948 crisis included candy for the children of West Berlin. Nice guy.

- Jerry Punch, a delightful, fascinating fellow accompanying one of his children on a field trip from Tennessee. A doctor by profession, indeed a national authority on emergency medical care (as I later learned by Googling him), he is also an on-air reporter for ESPN in football and NASCAR racing (twice saving the lives of drivers involved in crashes at the track). As we strolled along, I, a former sports reporter and lifelong fan, said I would like to have his job – and he, an avid student of history, said he would like to have my job. Jerry and I have a mutual acquaintance: Lou Holtz, who was a very cheerful assistant football coach at William and Mary in 1960 while I was the college's sports information director. Lou gave me the unoriginal but effective nickname which became popular among the coaches and the athletes: "Bear" Bryant!

- Doris Stearns Goodwin, whose masterful **Team of Rivals** (about Lincoln and his Cabinet) I had recently read. I went over to her, thanked her for her "magnificent contribution to our understanding of that beautiful man," and shook her hand. Enough said. Enough done.

- On the 12th of November 2000, a young Naval officer stationed in Norfolk brought me a group of seven impressive looking men in casual civilian attire – generals and colonels from the strategic planning staffs of former Soviet republics. The next day, they would be meeting for the first time with their NATO counterparts . . . Our two-hour tour lasted more than three hours. We had a lot to talk about, including politics – this at the time of the raging battle over Florida's presidential election results, which prompted a Romanian general to say gruffly while wagging his finger in a pleasantly chiding manner: "Remember, B . . . One man, one vote. Right?" I replied: "Well, that *is* the way the system is *supposed* to work."

- Not to mention Mr. Lincoln and Santa Claus . . . One day in the fort, I noticed a fellow who looked a lot like Abraham Lincoln, so I went over to him and said that he sure looked a lot like you-know-who, whereupon he cordially introduced himself (fully in character) as you-know-who. The guy's a professional re-enactor . . . One day on the loop, a day so slow there were no vehicles in the bus parking area, a big RV arrived and claimed a bus slot. Two colleagues and I, getting a fairly good glimpse of the man behind the steering wheel, noted his similarity to Santa Claus, which was amusing. Then the guy exited the RV, and he looked so much like you-know-who on vacation that as he walked toward us we suppressed with difficulty our laughter and lectured each other to be polite. With a hearty ho-ho-ho, he introduced himself as you-know-who – and we erupted in liberated laughter.

GROUPS

At least three groups – people I've been escorting annually for many years – merit special mention: Diane Smith and Lea Holmon and the other adults with the fifth-graders from the Dr. Mudd History Club at Samuel Mudd Elementary School in Waldorf, Maryland; Tracey Hickenlooper and her adult posse and their fifth-graders from the Seven Hills Doherty School in Cincinnati, Ohio; and Cathy Alderman and Steve Main and their students from Anderson New Technology High in Anderson, California.

Diane Smith

Doctor Mudd History Club

Greeting the adults with one of these groups after a year's absence is like a family reunion. The students are always ready for me, and expectations are high. I dare not disappoint them, or Diane, or Tracey, or Cathy.

I really admire Diane's extracurricular program at Mudd Elementary. The students have weekly meetings before school, go on monthly field trips ranging from Gettysburg to Yorktown, and in the spring conduct an annual Jeopardy-style game night at the school. (A couple of years ago, Diane sent to me at the Settlement a big scrapbook of photographs and descriptions of their previous year's journeys. When I opened the package, nearby MPAs became interested in the scrapbook, so a supervisor asked me to leave it on the counter for the rest of the week, which I was happy to do.)

My affection for Tracey and the other fine folks who always accompany Seven Hills Doherty is attributable not to the steady stream of inexpensive but priceless gifts they have bestowed on me during the years, or to the high honor they bestowed on me in making me an honorary member of the faculty. It is attributable to their niceness. (I shall discuss those "gifts" in a later chapter.)

My closest relationship has been with the folks from Anderson. Besides escorting them on tours at Jamestown and Yorktown and occasionally helping with local travel arrangements, I have met with them at their motel when their schedule allowed it, for continuing discussions of the world. Once, I accompanied them on a guided tour of Colonial Williamsburg, gaining an interesting perspective on several levels.

Thanks to the postal, telephonic and Internet connections between Williamsburg and Anderson, Cathy and her colleagues and I have been able to exchange thoughts regarding curriculum and methodology, and some of her students and I have discussed class projects requiring historical analysis.

Some months after our first encounter in 2004, Cathy sent me a nice note, and wondered if I remembered her and her group. I did, though vaguely, noting a fact which has resonated throughout my time as an MPA: "It is a truism of life as a teacher at Jamestown that one can form a genuine and strong friendship with a visitor likely not to be met again, or, if met again, likely not to be recognized. It is a bittersweet reality."

A decade ago, I didn't know Cathy Alderman and Steve Main existed. Today, Cathy and Steve are dear personal friends, as are Diane and Lea and Tracey and her posse. I have been blessed.

Postscript: After writing this, I got in touch with my once-upon-a-time debate partner Deliaan Angel Gettler, now living in Cincinnati, and sent her my manuscript. That's how I learned that Dee is closely connected to the Seven Hills Doherty School, which her children attended and her grandchildren now attend, and well acquainted with Tracey ("a talented and dedicated teacher"). Such a wonderful coincidence!

* * *

A year or so before it ceased being rumor and speculation that Barry Bonds was using steroids, I directly asked a high school group from San Francisco: "Is Barry Bonds using steroids?" The group, students and adults, chorally said yes – then began telling me *when* he began juicing. To them, it was common knowledge.

* * *

Soon after I began working at the Settlement, I learned that most of the students were well behaved and in a mood to learn, that it would be relatively easy and fun to teach them.

Then I had a group which far exceeded my expectations, so at the end of our tour I praised them for being so well prepared and eager to learn, for asking so many great questions, for being so nice. "Never underestimate," I said, "the power of nice." Then I impulsively created B's Top 10, told them they were the first group on the list, and said: "Consider it an honor. Give yourselves a standing ovation!" Which they did.

In time, of course, the Top 10 was filled to capacity, so I created B's Top 20, then B's Top 30, then B's Top 40. So far, approximately 50 groups have earned the distinction, for whatever it's worth, which I think is a lot, as do seemingly my honorees.

* * *

One fine June day, I escorted a squad of 15 high school cheerleaders from Kentucky. Fresh from winning a major regional championship in a tournament at the College of William and Mary,

238

they arrived in a great mood, ready for adventure. I promised I would give them my best tour if at the end of it they gave me their best cheer. They agreed – cheerfully, of course.

Two hours later, exiting the church, one of the girls asked: "B, is this the end of the tour?"

"Yes, it is."

Swiftly, with championship precision, the girls spread out, right there in the middle of the fort, and proceeded to give me the best darn cheer I ever did hear and see – a thank-you cheer, naturally.

* * *

On April 16, 2007, a gunman killed 37 people and wounded 17 others on the campus of Virginia Tech.

The flags at Jamestown Settlement and the Yorktown Victory Center were lowered to half-mast – at Yorktown the flag of the United States and the flags of the 13 original states, at Jamestown the flag of the United States and the flags of all 50 of the states – the Union, together in mourning.

Several days later, at Jamestown, I escorted half of a high school choir from Charleston, South Carolina. I told them I would give them a really good tour if at the end of it they would sing for me. They happily agreed.

At our last stop, in front of the light display near the statue of Opechancanough, one of the students asked: "B, is the tour over?"

"I suppose it is."

And they began singing – right there in the middle of the gallery – "Ave Maria" . . . so *very* beautifully . . . and I began to cry, quite freely.

When they were done, I composed myself somewhat and said: "You must pardon me . . . We have had a great tragedy in Virginia, as you probably know, and I have not yet grieved."

One by one, the students and their teachers, many of them also in tears, gave me a good hug.

Under the circumstances, it was a truly wonderful moment.

* * *

I have been fortunate. I have experienced very few significant disciplinary problems on my tours with school groups. In fact, I can recall only two occasions when, even as a tour was beginning, I felt the absolute necessity of drawing a line in the sand.

One day at Jamestown, near the Discovery Tower, I halted my high school group, turned around and (with two trouble-makers in mind) declared that I could not conduct a good tour under these conditions, that there would have to be better discipline, much better discipline. At that, two boys stepped confidently forward and stationed themselves with folded arms on either side of me (rather like white brothers of the Nation of Islam), promising to protect me. I consented, and the rest of the tour went very well, the two boys always quietly at my side. They were, of course, the original trouble-makers.

One day at Yorktown, entering the encampment, I halted my high school group of rowdy boys, turned around and sternly announced that from this point on there would be two groups. One group would continue with me. The other group would return (with an adult) to the bus and figure out how to explain to their teacher what had happened. No one volunteered for the second group. From that point on, the tour proceeded smoothly – and cordially, with no hard feelings.

Once, I did snap too harshly at a disruptive fifth-grader. I quickly apologized, to the boy and to the teacher, for losing my temper. But the teacher in a whisper commended me, saying it was the only way to deal with that child (who was not thereafter a problem).

* * *

I had just begun my tour with a group of about 25 adults (folks from several states brought together by a tour company) when I noticed some of them slipping away. Not a good sign.

As we reached the village, others promptly began slipping away, and I began to wonder why – and soon found out why those early deserters and most of the rest of the group had slipped away by the time the group (or what was left of it) reached the ships.

Why? Because on the tour were a man and his adult daughter, and as soon as I started trying to teach in the village the two of them began constantly interrupting and supplementing, demonstrating that they knew **everything**. The only problem: Everything they knew was **wrong**. I couldn't even begin to try to correct them, so ego-centered and oblivious of others they were, so swift was the flow of their misinformation, most of it created from thin air, much of it beyond absurd.

This continued throughout the tour, at the end of which only six people were still with me. Along the way, one of the brave few survivors apologized for the desertions and explained what didn't need explaining. He said the father and daughter had been spoiling the trip wherever the group went. I told him I fully understood. In fact, I wish I could have slipped away myself.

* * *

I have lost two groups, although I count only one of them as truly lost, and even then only briefly.

One day, on the loop, another MPA and I were waiting for a busload of middle schoolers when we were told that the group had arrived earlier, checked in, and headed out. So my colleague and I headed out, too, quickly, following their likely path through the gallery to the village to the ships to the fort, searching for a group about the right size and grade level. We never found them; as far as I'm concerned, *they* lost *us*. But the MPA and I had a wonderful time getting to know one another better.

Another day, at the ships, I led my group of Kentucky high school band members (an important fact to remember) up the stairs from the 'tween deck, turned left, walked along the side of the ship to the top of the gangway, turned right and proceeded down the gangway, then turned right on the pier, walked about 10 feet, and stopped, and turned around – and there was **nobody** behind me, not on the pier, not on the gangway, not along the side of the ship – **nobody!** Puzzled to the point of bewilderment, I retraced my steps, and found the answer. The band member directly behind me on the stairs, instead of following me and turning left, turned right and entered a cabin, followed obediently by the others. When I found them, almost all of them had crammed into the cabin – and, as in the parade scene in the movie "Animal House," the few outside were trying to get in! (This looks like my only opportunity to squeeze into the book one of my favorite quotations, from Daniel Boone, responding to an obvious question about his years of exploring the wilderness: "I can't say as ever I was *lost*, but I was *bewildered* once for three days.")

Drifting Memories

- During the week following 9-11, a contingent of subdued high school students arrived from Brooklyn. They had witnessed the whole thing from their school. The MPAs were especially sensitive and kind that day. The kids and teachers were especially appreciative.

- With groups of refugee children from war-torn places, we noticed many of them flinching at the distant sound of gunfire in the fort, so we reassured them; and when we entered the fort, we stayed well away from the musket demonstrations.

- A mostly deaf group of adult teachers of the deaf couldn't vocalize "B" so they signed it, with gusto, whenever (with the help of an interpreter) I asked.

- Special education groups, particularly students with severe physical and/or mental disabilities, sometimes represent a challenge which no MPA can adequately meet. But we try. Whenever I encounter a special ed teacher, I offer her or him a hug, which is invariably accepted. Such teachers are truly special. I love 'em.

- Twice within a month, I had groups of elderly white folks (most of them in their late 70s to early 90s) from churches in the Atlanta area. On both tours, the subject of Abraham Lincoln arose. I was so very pleased to hear my people expressing their respect and affection, even a degree of reverence, for the man. Very reassuring.

SELF-GUIDED

Self-guided (also known as misguided) groups can disrupt the best of plans. The problem doesn't seem as bad now as it once was. When it was at its worst, I expressed the frustration of all MPAs and interpreters in a memo to Karen Norako regarding the recent experience of my group of middle schoolers from Colorado:

I promised the group as we walked past the Susan Constant that we would be going on board in a few minutes, then moved to the map. A few minutes later, as we turned toward the Susan, we saw a large swarm of self-guided teenagers – at least a hundred of them and probably more – blocking the pier at the Susan, some of them already streaming aboard. My lead teacher and I quickly decided to go instead to the Godspeed, which we did. Soon, when we were down below, we heard a lot of noise topside; and soon, the self-guided people began pouring down the stairs into the middle of our group, and then more of them began coming down the other stairs, creating an unacceptable situation. I became increasingly concerned and annoyed, and I ordered the teenagers crowding the exit to turn around and go back up, which with difficulty they did. Topside, when I finally extricated our group, the teenagers were everywhere. On the pier, I felt compelled to apologize to the teacher, who was very understanding.

I was informed later that the teens were instructed not to board without an adult, but simply disregarded the instruction, in such numbers that nothing could be done about it. I suspect that the situation at the Susan was similar – because at no time did I see any adult with the teens.

It reminded me of two previous, particularly egregious instances of misconduct by large self-guided groups. I remember the day when a single adult led a mob of about 200 students onto the pier and declared: "All right, spread all over the ships!" They did, destroying the visitor experience on the pier for almost an hour. And I remember the day when I arrived to work and witnessed 5-7 busloads of self-guided teenagers noisily moving in one massive swarm across the lawn toward the village, with not one adult in sight. Later, as I led my group through the outdoor area, I learned of the chaos these people had caused.

The problem is obvious, and most of the blame should be placed not on the kids but on the tour companies and accompanying adults. The youngsters' expectations of this place, and their conduct while here, are determined by their adults.

We are a teaching institution, not an amusement park, and whatever problem significantly interferes with and distracts from our teaching mission should be substantially corrected.

* * *

It isn't always a disaster.

At Yorktown on a busy day, I was waiting with several other MPAs for our groups to arrive when three unexpected busloads of self-guided middle school students arrived. To get them started promptly but with some sense of order, to make room for our own groups and improve everybody's experience, we moved them to an area near the farm, and I stood on a bench.

I spoke rapidly for several minutes, welcoming them, telling them where they were and why, describing the museum, urging the adults to divide the students into small groups and go to different sites. Which, in a wonderful display of cooperation, they did.

Later, I heard no horror stories from the interpreters.

TEACHERS

On most days, which MPA gets which group is a matter of random selection, the luck of the draw.

Sometimes, I am requested in advance by teachers who have been with me in previous years, and this is arranged. Often, arriving teachers will ask for me or simply glom their groups onto me.

Occasionally, I must honestly if immodestly report, arriving teachers have "competed" for me. Usually, these disputes (in which I most definitely do not get involved) are settled quite amicably. Three contrary instances do come to mind, though I didn't witness one of them:

- "I had to fight to get Mr. B!" a teacher wrote on my evaluation.

- As I boarded a bus, two teachers exclaimed "B!" and began arguing over who was going to get me, one teacher winning the argument by declaring: "You had him last year!"

- On the patio, in a mob waiting for MPAs to be matched with groups, two teachers began

248

squabbling, one teacher ending the spat by summoning her group to her quickly, lightly bullying past the other teacher, and planting her group in front of me, announcing: "We're ready, B!"

* * *

Walking alongside a teacher toward the main entrance with our students following, we bumped into each other, each apologizing to the other. Then we bumped together again, and again mutually apologized. When we collided the third time, I stopped, turned to her and said: "Actually, I'm blind in my left eye."

She replied: "And I'm blind in my right eye."

We switched places.

Problem solved.

STANDARDS (AND SOURCES) OF LEARNING

As instructors at teaching institutions administered by the Virginia Department of Education, MPAs and interpreters re-enforce the Standards of Learning in our public schools, and we do a very good job of it, according to the classroom teachers and school principals who comment on our work.

One reason our SOL teaching is so effective is because we are not in a classroom, but in a more stimulating environment. Another reason is because we are not limited to or preoccupied with the SOLs, but are free to enrich the learning experience with additional knowledge, deeper discussions, broader understandings.

Based on the considerable grumbling I've heard, there is one issue which strongly, indeed fervently unites public school teachers and administrators throughout the United States – the overemphasis on rote learning and standardized testing at the expense of creative teaching and critical thinking.

It's hard enough nowadays to recruit, train and retain good teachers. The current system is discouraging a lot of bright and talented people from becoming teachers, and encouraging a lot of others to leave the profession, a decision painful for most.

The Virginia Association of School Superintendents (whose president until recently was my friend Steve Staples) has circulated among local school boards a resolution seeking a re-examination of the state's Standards of Learning, and scores of localities have endorsed it. The resolution begins by asserting that "the over-reliance on standardized, high-stakes testing as the only assessment of learning that really matters in the state and federal accountability systems is strangling our public schools and undermining any chance that educators have to transform a traditional system of schooling into a broad range of learning experiences that better prepares our students to live successfully and be competitive on a global stage." It argues that "imposing relentless test preparation and boring memorization of facts to enhance test performance is doing little more than stealing the love of learning from our students and assuring that we fall short of our goals."

I would be remiss in my professional obligation to the teachers I've met, and in my personal obligation to their students, if I failed to add my voice to the rising chorus appealing for fundamental changes in the current system.

* * *

In 2011, in the aftermath of protracted significant publicity regarding erroneous information about the Civil War in a state-approved third-grade history textbook published by Five Ponds Press, I reviewed all of the references to Nat Turner in all of the state-approved textbooks used in Virginia.

I shared my critique (which cited approximately 50 problems in fact or interpretation), together with an appeal for the state to prepare a teacher's guide on the subject, with the Virginia Department of Education and with the newspapers which had reported the Five Ponds story. Virginia's Superintendent of Public Instruction replied that my concerns would be considered in 2015. I replied that her answer was not satisfactory. The newspapers chose to ignore the matter.

In 2012, I shared with all of the public school superintendents in Virginia not only the textbook critique, but also a teacher's guide to the subject, which I shared with the Virginia Department of Education and the newspapers, which ignored it.

It is an unfortunate aspect of this Information Age in which we live that much of the information is incomplete, or misleading, or wrong, *really* wrong. Young people need to be guided toward critical evaluation and reliable sources of good information – which definitely does not in many circumstances include Wikipedia. (I googled Nat Turner, and found about 30 problems with Wikipedia's brief account – beginning with the very first word of the account: Nathaniel . . . To the best of my knowledge, nobody *except* Wikipedia has ever called him that.)

Postscript: This spring of 2014, Virginia got a new Superintendent of Public Instruction – my friend Steve Staples, an excellent educator. Huzzah!!!

* * *

There is a much larger issue here. It became apparent several decades ago that the American people were beginning to lose the community memory of their history – not just the names and dates and places in the textbooks, but the personalities of those names, the meaning of those dates, the importance of those places. Considering the consistently sad results of surveys among the people as a whole, I shudder to think about the level of history education – and understanding – among the members of Congress.

I had occasion to address this issue in a 2006 email to 13 students in California – "The Anderson People" – with this introduction:

I shall begin by expressing my great pleasure at being asked to comment on your project. Its premise – that there are certain important facts which should be common knowledge among the whole people, a shared, defining legacy – addresses a critical problem in our educational system, and in our society.

The onrushing flood of significant history and change in the past 60 years, so much more rapid and complex and immediately urgent, has caused a serious disconnection between our people and the more distant historical events, people, social movements and technological breakthroughs which truly defined and described the American character, supposedly so distinct and progressive and worthy of emulation.

To me, the re-education of the American people to the basics of our own history is one of the highest priorities of the continuing American

Revolution. I commend your effort in this direction!

Through the years, I have given much thought to how this "re-education" might be accomplished on a national scale. Experience has taught me to be confident that when I perceive a big problem, others perceive it, too; that somewhere people are not just thinking about it seriously but working on it as well, and making progress. Revolutionary conditions require and generate originality and ingenuity in thinking and action, tapping the innate strengths and talents of the people, at all levels of society.

I do know this: Reacquainting the American people with their shared legacy should be a very enjoyable process, at all levels of learning. Americans like history well taught, and a great many of them are hungry – especially in these uncertain times – to know more.

Footnote 1: One measure of our loss of national memory is the story of Nat Turner. In 1831, almost everyone in the United States knew the name. The impact of the insurrection was massive, altering the course of history. In black oral tradition Nat's War led to Abe's War. But for a variety of reasons the story of Nat and the meaning of the insurrection became more and more obscure and confused and scarily controversial, until today very few people know the name of Nat Turner and almost no one knows what happened in 1831 in Southampton. For the record: In my opinion as a student of history and revolutionary process, Nat is one of the 10 most influential people and the insurrection is one of the 10 most influential events in American history.

It is the critical "missing link" in understanding our transition from the Revolutionary War to the Civil War (which a lot of people at the time considered a second revolution); and someday, I pray, someone will have enough sense and passion to make a **responsible** movie telling the story. It should be a great movie, clarifying the issues, making our humanity and our history more understandable, helping us to heal and reconcile.

Footnote 2: The ultimate measure of our loss of national memory is this matter of the **continuing** American Revolution, a critical concept the Founding Fathers fully understood but has been mostly forgotten through the intervening years. Did you learn about it in school? I didn't. And American history didn't make sense to me until I did finally grasp the concept, which Archibald MacLeish brilliantly explained in an essay in the Washington Post on the 4th of July 1976, under the only two-page banner headline I have ever seen: "And Now for the Big Question: The Bicentennial of What?".

Afterthought: John D. Rockefeller Jr. invested so much of his wealth in the restoration of Colonial Williamsburg because he envisioned it as a living shrine to democracy, to serve the **continuing** American Revolution, the priorities of which guide

255

Rockefeller family giving to this day. Our revolution represents, as my friend Colin Campbell, until recently the president of Colonial Williamsburg, has so well expressed it, "an idea for all people, for all time."

MAYANS ET AL

In 1982, I was asked to speak to a class of fifth-graders at a local elementary school. I don't remember what my topic was. All I recall is that when I invited *any* questions, several students quickly asked about what was obviously weighing heavily on all of their minds as all of them leaned forward to hear the answer to: How bad was the war really? Would they be dropping atomic bombs?

Their fear was touchable. I was taken aback. So was their teacher, who clearly had no idea they were so worried.

Folks, it was the *Falklands War*! If you're old enough, do you even remember it or ever think about it? If you're not old enough, have you ever even heard about it?

But to those impressionable young people – and presumably to a great many other young people then being exposed to vivid television images and overheard conversations – it was something to be feared immediately and deeply. Their world was in crisis.

I put their minds at ease.

I mention the Falklands incident because on many occasions in recent years students have expressed a similar undercurrent of great concern about two things.

Thing 1: The Mayan calendar. It ended on December 21, 2012. The world didn't. Prior to that date, I was often asked about it. I answered by asking the questioner if he or she had a wall calendar at home. Sure. What's the last month? December. What's the last day? The 31st. So at midnight on the 31st, does the world end – or do you put up a new calendar? Duh. (Early in December of 2012, archaeologists announced a discovery completely debunking the doomsday notion!)

Thing 2: Asteroids. Yes, a big one hitting Earth would really ruin our day. But the odds are comfortably in our favor during the near future, and during the near future we can and should and really must develop and deploy an asteroidal collision avoidance system. To me, this should be the highest priority of the global democratic revolution; fortunately, it is also one of our more easily accomplishable.

SCENES ALONG THE PIER

Believe It or Not – Improbably, it happened down below on the Susan. On an uncommonly busy day, one group of high school students was beginning to climb up the exit stairs as another group of high schoolers began to pour down the entrance stairs, with two other groups of high schoolers in between – all or most of four groups down below at the same time – from four major cities in Texas!

Reliably Reported – A little girl preceded her father up the gangway onto the Susan. Midway, she jumped into the water, followed quickly by her father. Soon, both were on the pier.

Smiling, the father brushed off any concern or thought of filing an incident report. "Happens a lot," he said. "She loves the water."

Almost News Item – Leading my group of high schoolers up the gangway, I paused so their teacher could take a picture from the pier. Photo ops are very important.

The youngsters smiled and posed as teenagers do, and all of them leaned forward a little – and the gangway tilted *way* over, briefly a bit scary. Everyone got the message: End of Kodak moment.

Never again on the gangway!

Bathroom Humor – Not with my group, but an elementary school boy straggling behind his group leaving the 'tween deck on the Susan took the interpreter at his word and used the chamber pot for its intended purpose.

More Bathroom Humor – With my group of fifth-graders scrunched into a corner of the 'tween deck on a rather noisy day, I invited *any* questions –

having already told them that ol' B has a hearing problem so they had to speak loudly and clearly.

"B," asked a sweet girl sitting next to her father, "what did they use for toilet paper?"

I hesitated in answering, so her father, in a voice loud enough to be heard on the pier, said: "She said: What did they use for toilet paper?"

"I *heard* her," I laughed. "I just haven't figured out how to *answer* her!" So I did the smart thing – now here's a life-lesson for you – and said: "I don't know." (The beginning of wisdom is the recognition of ignorance.) Then I did another smart thing and asked a nearby interpreter the question, and she, put on the spot – or the hot seat, as it were – answered with the ease and expertise so rampant here: "Rags."

Alarming – On the pier at precisely 11:13 a.m., right on schedule, the annoying wailing began throughout the region likely to be most immediately affected by a serious incident at the Surry nuclear power station a few miles downriver.

A boy asked his father what that noise was. The father said: "Son, either they're testing the sirens . . . or soon we're going to be very warm."

Thrilling – The pier was busy as my group gathered on the main deck of the Susan, waiting to go below.

I watched (as I assumed at least a few other folks were watching) as two birds engaged over the cove in a mid-air duel over possession of the wriggling fish one of the birds held in its talon. The squabble

259

continued for a couple of minutes, until the fish, apparently tired of the ruckus, wriggled free and plunged into the river – and a great cheer arose aboard the ships and along the pier!

Enlightening – For some time, down below on the Susan, I had referred to the cannon and asked my groups: "Why were there cannon aboard a merchant ship? Who were the English afraid of?" (Answer: Pirates, to some extent, but mostly the Spanish.)

One day, having heard this for the first time, excellent Englishman and ships interpreter (and violin-maker) Dennis Parris came over to me as we were preparing to leave the 'tween deck, and he gently but firmly said: "Bill, the English were 'afraid' of **no one**." I who slept safely during the Battle of Britain nodded. I fully understood.

Since then, I have asked my groups: "Who were the English concerned about?"

Speaking of the Battle of Britain, I must add this footnote: I've been saying for a long time that if I ever met an RAF veteran of the Battle of Britain I would prostrate myself in front of him in gratitude, and I have mentioned it to a few adult groups. ("Never in the course of history," Churchill said, "have so many owed so much to so few.") In one group, an English lady said her father had flown for the RAF during that epic battle. "That's good enough for me," I said, kneeling, taking her hand

and kissing it lightly – a pittance of payment for a job well done.

Diane Smith
Jamestown Island

The dogmas of the quiet past are inadequate to the stormy present. The occasion is piled high with difficulty, and we must rise with the occasion. As our case is new, we must think anew and act anew.
Abraham Lincoln

CHAPTER 7: ALONG THE WAY

"WHAT DO YOU DO IN REAL LIFE?"

"I make popcorn," said the guy from Maryland in response to a question I often ask of parents and chaperones and other random adults on my tours. "For whom do you make popcorn?" I asked. "Ocean City," he said, with little need for elaboration, being the biggest maker of popcorn for one of the East Coast's most popular oceanside resorts.

"I blow up big things," said the cheerful fellow with the group of scientists and their wives from the Lawrence Livermore National Laboratory.

"I make chocolate éclairs and other things," said the baker lady, launching a necessarily brief but nonetheless mouth-watering discussion of how she makes **real** chocolate éclairs, the old fashioned way . . . and other things!

"Right now, nothing," said the rather young but

already very successful looking man accompanying his daughter's group. Once a practicing lawyer, he had created an Internet-savvy national network for legal services, had sold it, and now was wondering what to do with his millions. He had some good deeds in mind.

* * *

It is impossible to list all of the types of work performed by the people who have answered my casual question. It cannot be done. But just for the fun of it, I gotta try to give you to least a sense of the range of professional personalities from whom I have been privileged to learn stuff.

People in law enforcement – beat cops and sheriff's deputies and prison guards – plus firemen and emergency medical technicians.

Manual laborers and master craftsmen.

A whole lot of computer specialists, surprisingly few of them geekish.

Salesmen – real estate, insurance, all sorts of things.

Secretaries and corporate executives.

Government workers at all levels, including a few locally elected officials.

Lawyers, in many fields of the law, and paralegals.

Doctors, in many areas of medicine, and a comparable diversity of nurses.

Architects, developers, builders and men and

women in every one of the construction trades I know of.

Not to mention the teachers.

* * *

One day, a parent lamented the increasing politicization of the place where she worked. I asked where. "CIA headquarters at Langley." Don't ask me for more information than that. My lips are sealed.

In June of 2008, soon before the Democratic National Convention, a parent noted that her boss was so discouraged by the increasing partisanship and deadlock in Washington that he was considering leaving public life. I asked where she worked. "I'm the manager for Joe Biden's Wilmington office."

DIVERSITY

You see some of them for what they are – Orthodox Jews, Muslims, Sikh, Hindu, Amish – these and other people of many faiths, here for a common purpose, to learn and have a good time doing it.

You get to know a little about some people in bits and pieces of conversations overheard, just a few notes of music to one's ears. Foreigners. They're everywhere here. They come as individuals and couples and families small and large. They come in organized groups.

Sometimes, they come as contingents of military personnel (from dozens of nations) training at the Army Transportation Center at nearby Fort Eustis or at other military installations in the region.

Sometimes, they come as school students, from Mexico, the Pacific islands, France, Germany, Italy and elsewhere.

The Italians were from a high school in Pompei, near Naples, where my wife and I were married and lived for about nine months. I warmly greeted them in Italian but proceeded to teach in English, since they were not here to listen to me practice my often fractured Italian. They appreciated it when at the end I spoke again of my love of Italy, and quoted in Neapolitan from a plaque at the Castel dell'Ovo at the foot of Via Santa Lucia: "Cchiu luntano me staie, cchiu vicino te sento." It's hard to translate into English, but they understood. The further you are from me, the nearer you are to my heart.

I've escorted six adult groups from Russia, mostly teachers. I welcomed them in well rehearsed Russian, but stuck mostly with English the rest of the way. (It's like Dirty Harry said: A man's got to know his limitations.) Invited, I went with one group to the restored area of Williamsburg, ending our visit together at the Capitol. There, I spoke of the diversity of those earlier Americans, the challenge of working together, the revolutionary need to achieve . . . I paused, seemingly struggling to find the right word but actually waiting for one of them to supply it . . . A journalist from Moscow did: "Solidarity!"

CUBBIES ET AL

When I see a visitor nearby wearing a cap or sweater or game jersey telling me that he (or she) is a fan of the Washington professional football team, Virginia Tech or the University of Virginia, I usually call out: "Go, Redskins!" or "Go, Hokies!" or "Go, Wahoos!" The response is always positive. Fans are fans wherever they are.

I am especially fond of fans of the Chicago Cubs (among whom I included myself until my recent conversion to the Washington Nationals), and when I meet one I usually offer a sympathetic hug (always accepted), which, as any long-suffering Cubbie knows, is the appropriate gesture.

One spring day, leading my group away from the fort at tour's end, I saw a little old lady wearing a Cubbie cap slowly approaching. Encountering her, I offered her my hands, which she took into her hands, and I looked down at her and simply said: "Are they going to break our hearts again this year?" And with a brave smile on her sweet face, she looked up at me and said in a frail voice with sad resignation: "I'm afraid so." Nothing more needed to be said. We hugged, and went our separate ways.

Once, with a high school group from Chicago, I

began by asking who among them were Sox fans, and who were Cubbies. The students were about evenly divided. I noted that I was a Cubbie, and promised them a great tour. I gave them a great tour, too, one of my best – but the teacher who filled out my evaluation rated my skills and enthusiasm as only fair, requiring me to fill out a form explaining the low rating. I wrote simply that I could not explain it . . . Actually, there was a very good explanation – the only rational explanation – but I didn't expect my supervisor to understand it: The teacher must've been a Sox fan!

VETERANS

As I do with cops and firefighters and other folks in caring professions, I customarily offer a handshake to veterans whenever I can, thanking them for their service. The guys from World War II are invariably modest about it. "No problem (or) I was happy to serve (or) Just doing my duty." Yet if not for them . . .

One day, leading my group to the ships, I saw an ancient fellow sitting on a bench. He was wearing a Pearl Harbor Survivor cap. I approached him. "You were at Pearl Harbor, sir?" I gently asked. He replied: "Mi dispiace, signore, ma non parlo inglese." His daughter had bought the cap at a yard sale. Still, to me, he was a survivor of sorts.

RELIGION

It is a fact that among Jamestown's many better known distinctions it is also the first permanent Protestant Christian settlement in the Americas.

It is also true that the first item on the Virginia Company's list of mission priorities was to convert the native people (likewise a priority of other European colonizers in the so-called New World). MPA training provides good information on the subject.

Although it is not a major teaching point, considering how much else there is to teach, most of us do routinely refer to it, and all of us are or should be prepared to answer questions regarding it.

We are here to teach and explain history, not preach and explain religion.

* * *

One day, there was a stir at the Foundation. An out-of-state teacher at a Christian school had posted on the Internet a negative review of the Settlement, saying she had brought a group here once and had been told by her tour guide that he was not allowed to discuss the subject of religion, which she interpreted as anti-Christian, a suppression of knowledge. Not a good situation.

A few days later, I had a Christian school group whose teacher was – you guessed it maybe – the teacher who had posted the complaint. She identified herself at the beginning. I explained that her earlier tour guide was wrong, that we were fully willing, able and pleased to discuss the subject as part of the history. Our tour went quite well, ending in the church. The teacher was very satisfied, and said she'd be back, although I don't know if she ever posted a positive review.

* * *

Our museums are popular with religious schools – Protestant, Catholic, Jewish, Muslim – and I really enjoy my tours with their students and adults.

As a rule, their interest level is higher, their focus better, their mood more positive than with other school groups – and the behavior is consistently excellent.

Particularly with more fundamentalist Protestant schools (and many home-schooling parents), one must be especially sensitive at times. For example, some of the archaeological and geological information we cite, regarding the ancient dates of things, is at odds with the fundamentalist view of the age and nature of the Creation. I know there are teachers (and sometimes accompanying pastors) who must disagree with certain aspects of our teaching, and could object to it on the spot – but have never done so, a tribute to their courtesy and patience. (One lady did shake her head disapprovingly when I mentioned the age of some of the artifacts found at Cactus Hill. But that was all.)

* * *

At the end of a tour with fundamentalist middle school students, a group of mothers, several in tears, approached to thank me. "For the first time," one of them said, "we saw hope in our children's eyes! All they hear at church is doomsday."

This made me feel very good. I had succeeded as a teacher of history, because human hopes and dreams are what history is all about, whatever the religion.

* * *

In the church, I invited a fundamentalist group to ask questions, but their questions (all very good ones) soon moved beyond straightforward history toward sensitive areas of dogma, the questions increasingly requiring some degree of personal opinion.

Finally, for the only time in my experience, I stopped the questioning and said to the principal sitting in the back that I was becoming somewhat uneasy, that I would be happy to answer any questions but did not want to disrespect or offend their beliefs. The principal put me at ease. "You're doin' great, B! Just keep goin'!" I did.

"POLITICS" AND "REVOLUTION"

I am rarely asked if I have a political affiliation. Most folks comfortable enough with me to ask that

271

question already sense that I am politically independent. That is putting it mildly. In fact, I am fiercely independent – and in lockstep with the overwhelming majority of the American people extremely unhappy with both major parties.

I consider myself a radical moderate and believe in militant cooperation. Under pressure, I describe myself as a combination of Lincoln Republican and Truman Democrat. I once characterized my politics as so far to the left of Hubert Humphrey that I was approaching Richard Nixon from the right, and vice versa.

Essentially, I claim the right to be "conservative" on some issues, "liberal" on others and "centrist" on most, as well as the right to continue learning and if appropriate change my opinion. Someone once said that a wise man changes his mind; a fool, never.

I also claim the right to have friends all along the political spectrum. Good friends!

Responsible conservatism and responsible liberalism are legitimate and respectable, and necessary, appropriate to different degrees in different situations and circumstances. I admired Barry Goldwater as much as I admired Hubert Humphrey. Both men were thoughtful, honest, sincere, civil and deeply patriotic, devoted more to the people than to themselves or to special interests or uncompromising ideology.

To clarify further my "political" position and historical perspective, I mention that on the wall overlooking my workspace at home are the portraits of two men I especially admire – Abraham Lincoln and Jefferson Davis. Either I am very conflicted, or at peace, fully reconciled. You decide. (We were very fortunate during that terrible bleeding time. Lincoln, Davis, Grant and Lee were men of character and honor who by nature loved peace and hated war. If any one of them had been mean-spirited, we would be paying the price to this day.)

* * *

In contrast to the rarity of questions about my political affiliation, I am asked this question at least once on many of my tours: "What did you do before you began working here?" The first time I heard it, I hesitated briefly, then answered honestly. Since then, I have not hesitated: "The same thing I'm doing now. I am a full-time revolutionist, and this is part of my mission."

Most folks readily understand what I mean. The word "revolution" has bothered fewer and fewer people in recent years, because more and more they are understanding what the word means in the context of our times; almost no one is bothered by the r-word nowadays. Our political leaders grossly underestimate and/or ignore the intelligence and political sensibility of the American people. When so many people are willing, even eager to discuss the need for a revolution of some sort, any sort, it's time for the politicians to begin listening much,

much more closely.

The **reality** of American politics has been clear enough long enough that after less than a decade of being an MPA, among the people, I concluded that about 80 percent of our people are in basic agreement on about 90 percent of the critical issues, and yearn for consensus action, soon. They are becoming increasingly impatient. You probably don't need to be told this.

The American people aren't that badly divided – but the political parties and special interests and zealots of the left and right are, and it is to their advantage to divide the rest of us, by sowing seeds of distrust and anger among us, playing to our weaknesses, not our strengths. And people hate being used.

* * *

Mr. Lincoln advised: "Remember, to keep close to the people. They are always right, and will mislead no one."

What I am hearing from the people – people all across the political-social-economic-cultural spectrum – is an increasingly grumbling readiness for radical reform of our political process, to enable the true majority, the moderate center, to govern.

In recent years, numerous savvy syndicated columnists and political observers (and polls) have commented on the latent power of the people in the center, most recently Kathleen Parker: "What they

274

lack is organization and perhaps self-awareness. There really are enough of them to change the political climate – if only there were someone to harness and channel what I would call their normalcy."

The first phase of the American Revolution constructed the Union and imbedded our revolutionary ideals and process in the Constitution. The second phase, known as the Civil War, preserved the Union and advanced the ideal of human equality and opportunity. The third phase, in which we rather clearly are, requires us to rethink and reorganize our electoral system, no small task, but doable if the people will it. I am constantly giving some thought to how it might be done, and so are a lot of other folks!

Basically, we built the home we live in, we kept it from being subdivided, and now it's time do some renovation, some peaceful but very thorough housecleaning and structural improvement.

Footnote: I have occasionally seen, and perhaps you have seen, something called the "Congressional Reform Act of 2013," an Internet-circulating proposal wrongly attributed to Warren Buffett. If you're not familiar with it, google it. What's most interesting to me is that recently, within a four-day span, I received it in emails from a friend on the far left and a friend on the far right. Now, if **they** agree on the need for radical reform and have a consensus-oriented agenda in mind, there must be a lot of people in between them along the political spectrum who are sympathetic to the idea of reform and the development of a consensus agenda. (John Adams said that before the Revolutionary War began, the revolution itself "was in the minds and hearts of the people." What is in our hearts and minds today?)

5

* * *

Patrick Henry observed: "Honest men may honestly differ." Men and women of honor do not squabble like children in a sandbox – not while the world is impatiently waiting for us to act like grownups.

Let's face it, folks: Our national reputation, as a good people with good intentions, as the ideal example of effective, progressive democracy, is suffering. Honestly now, whatever your opinion of our domestic and foreign policy, do *you* think the world should be trying to emulate our current model of governance?

If we wish the world to see the benefits of democracy, to respect our example of what a free people can accomplish, we the people must prove, again, that we are worthy of the reputation which previous generations labored so hard and sacrificed so much to build.

My first wish
is to see this plague of mankind, war,
banished from the earth.
George Washington

People want peace so much,
one of these days governments had better
get out of the way and let 'em have it.
Dwight Eisenhower

Fighting not good.
Somebody always get hurt.
Mr. Miyagi

CHAPTER 8: REPORT CARDS

EVALUATIONS

Terms like "quality control" and "customer satisfaction" matter as much to the people at our teaching museums as they do to any sensible profession or institution dealing with the people. Particularly in the Historic Triangle, the term "visitor experience" has a special though hard to measure meaning.

Every tour and program (and there are 29 different types), whether with preschoolers or older folks, is evaluated by a teacher or leader of the group.

The evaluation form requests ratings – excellent, good, fair, poor, unable to judge – on the overall program, the quality of instructional skills, the instructor's rapport with the group, the hands-on experience. The interpreters are also rated.

Most teachers, bless 'em, really appreciate their Jamestown and Yorktown learning experiences, and they appreciate us. They respect our professional status and credentials. They know that we fully share their educational mission, and that most of us care about their kids almost as much as they do.

In discussing my own positive evaluations, I stress that they reflect not only my work, but also the work of many others. I expressed this feeling best in a note to a principal back in 2001: "Personally as well as professionally, I do appreciate your very thoughtful letter to Karen Norako. Being human, I am touched. Being a teacher, I am honored by your good opinion. As I said to you at Jamestown, any such praise of me is a reflection on all who work at that special place. Many people contribute to my confidence and enthusiasm, and by doing their own jobs well enable me to focus on doing my job well. We're a team. You understand."

After a tour at the Settlement, I overheard one teacher telling another that she would come back here for tours – "but not with that man!" On the flip side of the coin, a teacher wrote that he would return in the future – but "only with Mr. B!"

Occasionally, a teacher's appreciation is excessive, such as: "Our guide was absolutely the greatest, most awesome, finest, most enthusiastic and knowledgeable we believe we could have had!" Believe me, I wasn't that good; nobody here is **that** good.

Some nice comments: "If I was closer than Alaska, I'd have him in my classroom every semester" . . . "You seem to me the type of person with whom I would love to sit and chat" . . . "Would love to spend a week or so with him" . . . "Clone B! He needs to give tours at New Jamestown at the Bill 'B' Bryant Welcome Center."

Way back in 2001, when I was still wasting time wondering how much longer I would be working as an MPA, Karen Norako passed along to me an encouraging letter she had received from a principal praising her school's whole experience at Jamestown. The principal noted that at various museums she had never found a guide "who was able to make you feel like you were there and so was he. Mr. B was able to do just that. In his special way, he gave each one of us a Jamestown 'jewel' that we were able to bring back with us. Young people very quickly forget people they meet only once, but you must know that the students are still talking about Mr. B."

One lady added to her evaluation this comment: "To: Jamestown Foundation . . . **Keep Bill Bryant** on staff at **all costs**. He has inspired 16 young learning-reluctant Virginians today to want to **know more**." She also noted: "One of my girls said to me, 'I like history now!' after today's experience (& I've tried all year)."

Another lady observed: "Mr. B cherishes our world & all who live in it. The knowledge he imparts comes from first his heart. He is a treasure!"

* * *

Probably the most generous (and embarrassing) evaluation I've received came from a Utah teacher who created the rating of "perfect" in answer to five questions, circling it each time.

Then she wrote: "No government evaluation form could rate the knowledge and teaching this man has passed on to us. This man, if not already, should be the executive director of this facility. We are all better people because we have all met B."

Elsewhere on the form, she wrote: "In the movie 'Star Trek' Spock said it best – as he was poisoned by radiation – 'The needs of the many outweigh the needs of the few or the one.' B is concerned about the future of the many and not so much himself."

Then, to get me in trouble with my boss, she sketched on the back of the form a new organizational chart for our facility, with B as executive director and "everyone else taught by him" reporting to B. (Note to Phil: I have no designs on your job. You're doing just fine, as I've told you many times.)

* * *

Perhaps my most prized evaluation came in November of 2010 from Lisa Petrey-Kirk, whose Kentucky eighth-graders I taught at Jamestown one day and at Yorktown the next day.

Lisa, a bright and jovial lady whose students adored her, rated my instructional skills "super" and called me an "excellent teacher" and cited my enthusiasm as "an example of excellence."

I learned at Yorktown that Lisa was Kentucky's 2010 Teacher of the Year, and that she had very recently been to the White House for a formal reception honoring the nation's top teachers. So her opinion had a bit more weight than most. Yes, we hugged, wholeheartedly.

* * *

So much for the positive evaluations. Now for the negative.

There's not a lot to write about, actually, because there's little of it.

I have never been comfortable filling out what's called a "program information sheet" to try to explain a teacher's "fair" or "poor" rating, partly because it puts me or any MPA in a defensive mode, which might require criticizing the teacher and/or students; partly because sometimes the MPA doesn't have a clue as to what the teacher was thinking, particularly when the MPA thinks it was a pretty good tour; and partly because even when the MPA knows the explanation (like the Sox-loving and/or Cubbie-hating lady from Chicago who didn't like one of my best tours), it still doesn't seem rational or credible.

Rarely, the teacher is right. One teacher rated my enthusiasm "fair" – and I agreed with her, and said so on the program information sheet.

I remember well the morning I came back into the office so angry at the conduct of the teacher with my group that I refused to fill out a program information sheet, because I did not want to put into writing what I was thinking and feeling at that moment. Karen Norako "debriefed" me, taking copious notes. She was very understanding.

* * *

My worst evaluation came from not one but two teachers with an out-of-state group, actually half of a contingent of middle schoolers. Another MPA got the two men teachers and the boy students. I got the two women teachers and the girl students.

We had a good tour. The girls were quiet (in an odd way almost too much so), but very interested and attentive. The teachers, who seemed already unhappy when they arrived and were unsmiling and unengaging throughout, were very inattentive, not participating in most activities, standing well apart from the group, talking. I wondered how they could possibly fill out an evaluation sensibly.

I didn't realize until I returned to the office that the two teachers (and when an evaluation is done by committee it's usually not a good sign) had given me not one, not two but a record-setting three bad ratings, adding comments about the lack of student interaction, my delivery (of all things!), my failure to hold the students' interest and attention, my "fair" enthusiasm (really!) . . . I later learned that the two teachers, to the great embarrassment of their male colleagues, had been "difficult" during their whole field trip. I won't go into the details.

If this story didn't have a positive lesson in it, I wouldn't be telling it. My most vivid memory of that tour, a truly wonderful memory, has nothing to do with those teachers, and everything to do with their students – because, frankly, I would rather have the good opinion of the students than the teachers any day, and the bottom line is that I have never had a tour badly rated by a teacher that wasn't apparently well regarded by the students.

Here's what I wrote on the program information sheet on that particular occasion: "At end of tour,

283

about half the students suddenly offered me money. Lou Roehr said it seemed spontaneous, and that he had 'never seen anything like it.' Students were very nice, very appreciative."

Those sweet girls weren't offering me dollar bills, either. At a quick glance, while I ever so politely declined, it looked like well over a hundred dollars.

But it's not about the money, is it?

FEEDBACK

Quite aside from the formal evaluation process, informal evaluation usually begins during the tour, when a child says he or she is having a good time, thank you, B, or an adult compliments the job I'm doing.

Leaving the fort near the end of a tour with a really appreciative group from a school in remote western Virginia, I overheard a fifth-grade boy declare: "This is the bestest tour I've ever been on." His classmate said: "This is the *only* tour you've ever been on." The boy replied: "It's still the bestest!"

The scenes at the end of our tours can be and often are heart-warming, which is honestly the best way to describe it. I love watching my MPA colleagues being surrounded, applauded, cheered, hugged by thankful students and teachers, and I love it when I'm the center of such approving attention. No sense denying it.

Quite recently, near the end of my own tour, I watched relatively new MPA Fred Crosby being overwhelmed by a mob of elementary school kids. When I mentioned it to him the next day, he beamed. "I've been hugged by one or two kids before," he said, "but those kids were all coming at me. It felt like they were trying to take me down, like on a football field." Fred paused, still beaming. "It made *my* day, that's for sure." Fred retired a couple of years ago as an Air Force master sergeant with 20 years of service.

Only one group (out-of-state high schoolers) in my memory ever just disintegrated at the end, with not a single student or adult saying one word of thanks. I got a good formal evaluation, but it meant nothing to me. That final scene depressed me.

At Yorktown, as I walked toward my car after yet another pleasant tour with fifth-graders from a Catholic school in Virginia Beach, a parent walking toward their bus called out: "B! You probably don't know this, but you're a legend at our school."

At Jamestown, as I headed out with a group, a departing teacher called out: "B! – You had my class last year, and they talked about you all . . . year . . . long!"

* * *

I had seen the man before, several times, once on one of my tours. I figured he was with a tour company. He offered me his hand. I took it. "I've been in this business for 20 years," he said, shaking my hand vigorously, "and you're the best damn tour guide on the East Coast!" I thanked him. (My first thought afterward was how neat it would be to have a TV reality show featuring tour guides at various museums, from coast to coast. I still like the idea a lot.)

* * *

Then the cards and letters start coming in.

It's commonplace in the office for an MPA to share a nice thank-you message from a teacher or a whole class of students. After 15 years, I have three thick file folders of such messages, not to mention several packets too large for a file drawer and the massive (400-square-inch) folded card from some third-graders. One of the packets contains 22 distinctly different, very creative thank-you cards.

It's important to pass along to our interpreters comments really directed at them, such as: "You're not crazy like Jim," a boy wrote. The next time I saw Mr. Harrison, I told him what the boy had written, and we had another good laugh.

One teacher asked her students to pick the favorite part of their Jamestown experience. I got a few votes, but lost to Vince Petty the blacksmith in

286

a landslide. I told him so. Said I would've voted for him, too, and I meant it.

In response to a thank-you card in 2000, I wrote to "my friends in Herndon" this:

Thank **you**!

Following our time together at Jamestown Settlement, I picked up my wife at her workplace – and immediately told her all about the exceptionally wonderful group I had just been with. I told her I felt that I had given one of the very best tours I had ever given (and the number I've given is approaching 200), an accomplishment which requires inspiration, which you provided. It has been my experience within the learning process that students can be better than their teachers, but that teachers are only as good as their students. And you folks were great!

Then I received your card – also exceptionally wonderful – and immediately shared it with several of my co-workers, so they could feel the warmth of a praise which all the dedicated teachers at Jamestown Settlement richly deserve. I subsequently shared your card with my wife, too, of course.

Thank you so much for your generous expression of a respect, and an affection, I now sincerely express to you. The future, as I indicated to you at Jamestown, is going to be a challenging and exciting time – and you young people certainly seem to have the right attitude for making the most of it, the right way.

Cultivate your understanding and appreciation of history, beginning with current events, the history we're making nowadays, because it's important for you, as good citizens, to be well informed, so you can make intelligent decisions. And explore the past with real enthusiasm, knowing how much it matters to you even now, beginning with the history of your own family, community, state and nation. As you can, expand your interest to embrace the world . . . And do pay attention to the emerging future! The more you know about where we've been and where we are now, the easier it will be for you to understand and appreciate where we're going. That makes good sense, doesn't it?

I naturally hope you'll return to Jamestown (particularly as 2007 approaches), and that you'll become as well acquainted with Williamsburg and Yorktown. I've lived here for more than 40 years, and I'm still learning interesting new stuff, almost every day!

Thanks again for our time together, and for your thoughtful and delightful card, which I shall treasure.

I am your very good friend . . . B!

* * *

A few examples of nice notes:

"Now my favorite letter is B!"

"You made me wonder about the future."

"When I see New Jamestown I will think of you."

"I am now an optimist."

"You make me feel Virginian pride, and I'm not Virginian."

"When I came to Yorktown, I was saying in my head 'Oh no, not another tour.' But when we started, I was totally into it, and without you, I think I wouldn't have listened as well, or at all."

* * *

On one memorable occasion, three MPAs "evaluated" a school, in this email to teacher Gretchen Stott:

Greetings!

When my friends Mary Barlow and Bob James and I met in the office following our tours with Courthouse Road Elementary, we immediately began talking (somewhat excitedly) about our experiences, which were identical – and so positive that we agreed that we should let you know how impressed and pleased we were. All three groups were prepared, receptive, attentive, orderly, polite, nice – "the whole package," Mary said.

Mary, Bob and I are veterans at what we do, which means we have met many groups from many places. When all three groups from one school shine like yours, we know that something special is happening at Courthouse Road, and we want to encourage all of you – students and teachers alike – to keep up the great work! You make our job a joy. Please share our sentiments with your students and teachers, and with your principal.

Thanks for a wonderful experience.

INFLUENCE

Teachers influence students. That's a teacher's job. We *exist* to help pass along to younger human beings the accumulated knowledge, understanding and wisdom of our species, to help them become better people, capable of responsibly pursuing happiness not only in the changing world around them, but also in the world emerging. (One mustn't forget that bad or inadequate teachers also influence students, if only by limiting their abilities and their imagination.)

Good teachers *want* to influence students, as many as possible as much as possible. It is an inherent professional expectation, a simple human hope, sometimes only a prayer. But it's a conscious will. (A teacher said I belonged in a classroom. I asked her how many students she had in a year.

"About 25," she said. "I average 4,000," I said, deliberately including adults. She nodded.)

* * *

It made me smile when a student wrote: "Thanks. The tour was awesome. My favorite part was meeting you! You rock!" The experience was obviously positive.

But it made me think hard when a teenager wrote: "For as little time I had with you, you completely changed the outlook of my life. I promise I will spread a little of your wisdom around."

And it made me think harder when a fifth-grader wrote: "You have changed my whole life forever." What exactly did I say or do to cause that effect?

"I loved how you said one person can make a difference," a Californian wrote. "I believe that now, because you **proved** it." How, exactly?

At least, when a gaggle of excited teenagers promises to "make B famous in Wisconsin," it won't be as a bad guy. I hope.

* * *

Still waters can run very deep indeed. The shyest boy or girl in a group, the one who never says anything or seems to react to anything, might be the one who rushes toward you at the end of a tour and gives you the first big hug. I operate on the assumption that every person in my group is always listening raptly to every word I say, because sometimes at least one person is, obviously or not.

Sometimes, the waters run visibly, rapidly. When a whole group is manifestly eager for adventure and hungry for understanding, and clearly capable of handling higher-level learning, I give it to 'em. When only a few people are especially eager and hungry, or even only one person, I put some food on the table for the whole group knowing only a few, or one, will fully appreciate the taste.

Some extremely intelligent young people haven't yet figured out how to be extremely intelligent and true to one's self without being bothersome or obnoxious to other people. When I can, I gently offer a little advice about how to ask and/or answer questions and demonstrate superior knowledge without seeming personally superior to others, how to be a bit less assertive, less obtrusive, more patient, more understanding and respectful of others.

* * *

Three young people, two from overseas, seemed already far beyond my possible influence, but still I made gestures.

At Jamestown, asked what she wanted to be when she grew up, a girl very confidently answered:

292

"The President of South Africa." At Yorktown, asked the same question, a boy with certainty replied: "I want to be the Chancellor of Germany!" I wished them success in their ambition, and urged them always to respect and serve the people.

At the end of a tour at Yorktown, I felt compelled to say something to a middle school girl who oddly had captured and held my own attention throughout the tour. It wasn't something she had said or done, because she hadn't said or done anything unusual. But she had a certain poise and grace. She was fully attentive, keenly focused, clearly intelligent and mature beyond her years. And wherever we went on site, her classmates, who obviously liked her as much as she seemed to like them, naturally, quietly deferred to her, made room for her, eased her path. I had never seen anything quite like it, so at the end I approached her, saying simply: "You are special, aren't you?" She smiled a very slight, modest, thoughtful smile, and said: "Yes." I needed only to remind her (for I am sure she had already thought of it) to respect and serve the people, and she needed only to nod.

Footnote: One can deliberately plant a seed which yields utterly unexpected fruit. Having written the High Frontier position paper being circulated in Congress and at the White House, I felt a citizen obligation to respect the democratic process and try to educate my own member of Congress, so I requested an opportunity to meet with Representative Paul Trible at his district office in Newport News. I was granted only 15 minutes, not a lot of time to explain a cosmic concept. Paul was busy with his paperwork and disinterested at first, but soon began taking notes; and when precisely at the end of my 15 minutes I got up and headed toward the door, he got up and accompanied me, asking questions. A week or so later, in Williamsburg, I spent a couple of hours with two of Paul's assistants, briefing them in great detail. Armed with this new information, Paul worked with Newt Gingrich to organize the Congressional Space Caucus, which instead of promoting the peaceful purposes of the High Frontier focused on the Strategic Defense Initiative, which might or might not have been the tipping point in the Cold War but definitely had the negative effect of blunting the momentum of the High Frontier movement by diverting political and scientific attention and vital research funding. Such is the extent of my contribution to the fall of the Berlin Wall and the collapse of the Soviet Union.

Footnote to the footnote: Subsequently a member of the United States Senate, in 1996 Paul became president of Christopher Newport University in Newport News. Since then, he has led a remarkable transformation at the school named in honor of the one-armed mariner who brought the 104 English settlers safely to landfall at Jamestown.

An entirely different footnote: I learned long ago that one can plant a seed without knowing it. When I was a senior in high school, one of my buddies was a lively bright sophomore named Ben Jones. I lost track of Ben until he emerged as Cooter on the original "Dukes of Hazzard" and then became a member of Congress from Georgia. Our mutual friend Patsy Weigel later informed me that I had helped to influence Ben to go into acting and into politics. I was very pleased to hear this. It meant, among other things, that I had played a small role in that dramatic scene in 1991 when Ben and two other members of Congress went to Tiananmen Square in Beijing, placed flowers on the so recently bloodied pavement, and unfurled a three-foot banner saying in Chinese and English: "In memory of those who died in Tiananmen Square."

Leah Holmon

Diane Smith and B

$$$

FULL DISCLOSURE

As an employee of the people and the Commonwealth of Virginia, I cannot accept gratuitous financial remuneration – tips – merely for doing my job. I more than wholeheartedly agree with this policy. Any state employee – a lowly part-timer like me or a highly elected official – who gains financially from the performance of public service violates the essence of the Virginia way.

Having said that, I now make full disclosure, itemized:

1

Although I have politely declined offers of money, I did politely accept a $10 bill from a nice man at the end of a Visitor Services tour. I initially resisted, explaining our policy, but he interrupted me: "You don't understand. This isn't for you. This is to buy ice cream for your grandchildren. Now take it!"

I confess: I took it. The man was so nice, and so insistent. It would have been unpardonably impolite not to take it. The kids enjoyed the ice cream!

If as a result of the publication of this book I am required to write a check for $10 payable to the Commonwealth, I shall do so.

2

As for the approximately $1.50 (mostly in pennies and nickels and dimes) I accepted from students and adults wanting to help fund my "lucky penny" routine, I am likewise prepared to convey this sum to the Commonwealth, although I shall want it stipulated that every penny (and nickel and dime and the Kennedy half-dollar from the sweet little old lady to whom it was probably a keepsake) contributed to that worthy cause was spent for its intended purpose.

3

Then there's the nonmonetary stuff:

The "B" key ring bought for me at Michie's Tavern in Charlottesville by two boys with a group returning home, then mailed to me.

The deck of playing cards used at the Texas Station casino, a formal gift from Las Vegas high schoolers.

Boy Scout patches from groups going to or coming from jamborees.

Traditional trinkets from the Russians.

And the steady stream of little thank-you gestures from the folks at Seven Hills Doherty – the T-shirts, the water bottle, the pen, the key ring, the lanyard, the kitchen magnet, the softball game jersey as an honorary member of the faculty – all clearly marked with the school's name.

4

Finally, there's the Polynesian incident.

Perhaps my favorite student group of all time, from anywhere, came from several western Pacific islands, many of the youngsters wearing what I later learned were kukui-nut leis, some emblazoned with sea turtles. Even more so than most groups traveling here from distant places, these kids were *so* appreciative of the whole experience, and *so* nice.

As we assembled at the end, a boy approached, took off his lei, said I reminded him of his recently deceased grandfather, and placed it around my neck. Another boy approached, took off his lei, said I reminded him of his grandfather and that he was going to tell his grandfather all about me when he got home, and placed it around my neck. Much hugging. Great kids.

* * *

Here's the deal: If as a result of the publication of this book I am required to surrender these "gifts" (or whatever you might prefer to call them) to the Commonwealth, I shall with the greatest reluctance do so – except for the leis. They are **mine.**

Indeed I tremble for my country
when I reflect that God is just,
that his justice cannot sleep forever . . .
Thomas Jefferson

FOOTNOTE: NAT TURNER

Rather late in the process of composing this book, I have decided to add this questionably relevant section, because (1) I can, since this is my book, and (2) I should, since this is an opportunity to share with more people the very important story of the Southampton Slave Insurrection of 1831.

As noted in Chapter 6, in 2011 I submitted to the Virginia Department of Education a critique of all references to Nat Turner in the state-approved textbooks used in the public schools. The then-Superintendent of Public Instruction replied with a bureaucratic nonresponse, which did not please me. . . This is how I replied:

I am very disappointed and concerned by your letter, which clearly states that the problems I cited in my critique will not be considered until 2015 and clearly implies that nothing will be done in the meantime, that this misinformation will be allowed to stand, unquestioned.

As an educator and as a Virginian who cherishes history, I consider your response quite inadequate and unacceptable.

While I appreciate your detailed explanation of the textbook-approval process (with which I am already familiar), that explanation is irrelevant to this discussion.

I have shared my critique with others, including the Williamsburg-James City County school system, which, to its great credit, has already decided to take appropriate action, informing its teachers of the problems in the textbooks used in the system. This action was explained to the Williamsburg-James City County School Board at its meeting on the 18th of October, in the context of the Five Ponds Press situation. Board members expressed interest in your response to what I sent you, so I shall be sharing your letter and this letter with the School Board, and with the others who have received the critique.

At the very least, the Virginia Department of Education could communicate these textbook concerns to the school divisions. Ideally, VDOE could arrange the preparation and

302

distribution of the teacher's guide I suggested. If VDOE cannot or will not do this, I can and shall.

We both want what is best for Virginia's students and teachers, and we can certainly do better in teaching this subject.

Sincerely . . . Bill Bryant

Likewise as previously noted, in 2012 (as promised) I prepared a teacher's guide and shared it with all of the public school superintendents in Virginia. I now share it with you – with the understanding that it is only a guide, only an outline of a much more complex and interesting story than a mere guide can tell. I can only hope, like any teacher, that you will want to learn more.

This document is not copyrighted, and may be reproduced, preferably with credit to the author.

Nat Turner
and the
Southampton Slave Insurrection of 1831

Prelude

The fear of insurrection has haunted slave-holding societies throughout history, as it did in the Americas when the European nations staked their colonial claims and began importing slave labor from Africa.

On August 20, 1791, the nightmare became reality in Haiti when slaves led by Toussaint L'Ouverture initiated an era of uprisings in Europe's Caribbean and South American colonies.

In Virginia on August 30, 1800, following months of preparation, slave Gabriel Prosser assembled a force of approximately a thousand men and led them toward the armory in Richmond – not knowing that the plot had been betrayed and that Governor James Monroe was leading a force of more than 650 militiamen to confront the insurgents. Suddenly, a massive storm erupted, violent rains flooding the roadways and washing away the bridge separating the approaching armies. The blacks then learned of the betrayal, and dispersed.

Some 36 of the plot's leaders were tried, convicted and executed by hanging, including Prosser, who had escaped as far as Norfolk before being captured. Governor Monroe noted that the condemned men "have uniformly met death with fortitude," and John Randolph observed: "The accused have exhibited a spirit which, if it becomes general, must deluge the Southern country in blood. They manifested a sense of their rights, and contempt of danger, and a thirst for revenge which portend the most unhappy consequences."

Prosser was hung on October 7, 1800. Fears of a general insurrection subsided.

On October 2, 1800, Nat Turner was born in Southampton County, Virginia, the son of a slave father and an African-born mother, Nancy, who tried to kill her baby soon after his birth, reportedly saying she did not want her child to be raised a slave.

Nat was born the property of Benjamin Turner, who with his family and slaves farmed in the sparsely populated countryside southwest of the Nottoway River and Southampton's only town, Jerusalem.

An ardent Methodist, Benjamin arranged for preachers to visit the remote neighborhood, which had no church, and encouraged his slaves to be religious. He brought in teachers to tutor his own children and others in the area, and many of his slaves also learned to read and write, and reckon numbers.

As a young child, Nat easily learned to read and write, and began displaying an uncommon intelligence which impressed whites and blacks alike. For this and other reasons (including certain markings on his skin which in the African tradition were seen as spiritual signs of great favor), some blacks said the boy might become a prophet, and he overheard his parents saying he was "intended for some great purpose."

Nat's father ran away, his identity and fate unknown.

Nat's white friends during childhood included Benjamin's son John Clark Turner and the Francis children – Sally, Salathiel and Nathaniel. A likely acquaintance was Dred Blow, a young slave who lived on a farm several miles away, near Bethlehem, until his master moved away from Southampton.

Benjamin Turner died late in 1810, very soon after deeding the land for a new neighborhood church (to become known as Turner's Meeting House). Most of his estate, including eight of his 30 slaves, became the property of his oldest son, Samuel.

Growing up, Nat worked more in the fields, but he also developed skills as a general handyman, mechanic and carpenter. In spare time, he experimented with casting metal into earthen molds and tried to make paper and gunpowder.

As he approached manhood, he became increasingly preoccupied with religion, acquiring his own Bible and devoting much time to reading it and meditating, sometimes at his secret place inside the Cabin Pond swamp. It seemed natural when he began preaching among the slaves and free blacks on neighboring farms. A woodland clearing became his regular preaching place.

During this time, he later claimed, he began experiencing revelations in which the Spirit convinced him he was "ordained for some great purpose in the hands of the Almighty."

Early in 1822, Samuel Turner died. Nat's mother Nancy, who had strongly influenced her son, remained with Samuel's widow. Nat was sold to Thomas Moore, whose wife Sally Francis had been Nat's friend since childhood. The slave Cherry, who would become Nat's wife, was sold to Giles Reese, whose farm was not far from Moore's.

Placed under an overseer, Nat ran away. He stayed away 30 days, then came home because, he later claimed, the Spirit had told him he "should return to the service of my earthly master."

Nat Turner married Cherry Reese. They would have three children.

During the summer of 1822, a widespread insurrectionary plot led by free black Denmark

Vesey in Charleston, South Carolina, was betrayed before it could happen on July 14, Bastille Day. Vesey and 34 other leaders were hung, the prosecutor declaring: "There is nothing they are bad enough to do that we are not powerful enough to punish."

During the 1820s, when not working, Nat moved freely through the countryside in his expanding ministry, becoming better known and more widely influential among the blacks. To whites and blacks, he became known as a man who never drank, never cursed, never stole, rarely carried any money, and always carried his Bible – and as a man who claimed to experience strange visions, which inspired some blacks but troubled some whites.

In 1825, history repeated itself at the Black Creek Meeting House in Southampton. In the pulpit in 1784, pastor David Barrow had denounced slavery, then freed his own slaves and moved to Kentucky, where in 1798 he published a widely circulated attack against slavery. On Christmas eve 1825, in the same pulpit, pastor Jonathan Lankford denounced slavery. He was soon replaced.

The idea of emancipation – with or without compensation to the owners or transportation back to Africa – had supporters among the whites of Southampton, the county's unusually large number of free blacks a result of earlier efforts by some Methodist and Baptist preachers and Quakers, before the Methodists and Baptists of the South began moving toward an accommodation with slavery. There was also some local support for the American Colonization Society, which in 1824 transported 70 Southampton free blacks to the new land in Africa.

In about 1827, Nat created a controversy. Having counseled a harsh overseer who "ceased his wickedness," Nat and the white man, Sally's uncle Etheldred Brantley Jr., asked to be baptized at Turner's Meeting House. The church's elders (headed by Sally's brother Nathaniel) decided against it. Nat then arranged for a public baptism, and on the chosen day, in the waters of Person's Mill Pond, the slave and the overseer baptized one another in the presence of many people, some of them very disapproving.

On another occasion, he reportedly attracted attention by declaring that the slaves should be free and someday would be.

Early in 1828, Thomas Moore died, and Nat became the property of Sally's young son Putnam. Nat also became an overseer on the farm.

On May 12, 1828, as he later claimed, Nat experienced a vision convincing him that his great purpose was to liberate his people, the Spirit telling him to await a sign in the heavens and meanwhile conceal from others the knowledge of his plan. Nat did reveal it to his wife Cherry.

In October of 1829, Sally married Joseph Travis, who moved in as new head of the family. In 1830, their son was born.

In 1830, Doctor John Floyd became governor of Virginia, determined to do whatever he could do to promote the idea of general emancipation, eventually to end what he believed to be Virginia's economically harmful reliance on slave labor.

During this time, Joseph and Sally Travis were visited by a young niece from a neighboring county. Back home, Lucy Travis wrote a letter in which she remembered Nat as a humble and kind Negro who enjoyed privileges almost equal to the whites.

Also during this time, Sally's brothers Nathaniel and Salathiel began cautioning her not to trust Nat, but to be wary of him.

According to the national census of 1830, the population of Southampton County was 16.074, including 6,543 whites, 7,756 slaves and 1,745 free blacks. Approximately 175 people lived in Jerusalem, site of the county's courthouse, jail and rarely used place of execution, the hanging tree.

Early in January of 1831, another boatload of Southampton free blacks departed from Norfolk for Africa. Among the passengers was a boy named Anthony Gardner.

And in January if not earlier, awaiting a clear sign in the heavens, Nat probably learned it was coming before it happened, along with other people able to read the stories and understand the graphics in the newspapers and new almanacs precisely predicting an eclipse of the Sun on February 12. The eclipse would be visible in its totality only along a line passing directly over Southampton.

On February 12, the Moon passed between Earth and the Sun. Over Southampton, the eclipse began at 10:50 a.m. and peaked at 12:25 in a peculiar cold twilight – a perfect circle of flames spectacularly dancing around the black Moon. The phenomenon ended at 1:53. Throughout the eastern United States, people were in awe, and many were fearful. Nat considered it the sign he had been awaiting, and immediately shared his mission of insurrection with four men he trusted most: Hark Travis, Henry Porter, Nelson Williams and Sam Francis. Initially, the men planned to begin the uprising on July 4, but the date passed without action, the conspirators continuing to form and reject plans. Nat could not know how well the secret was being kept.

Meanwhile, unreported in American newspapers, from mid-July into early August, great volcanic eruptions happened in the Philippines and in the Mediterranean, columns of ash reaching high into the atmosphere, spreading around the world with the winds. The resulting unexpected solar phenomenon eventually reached Southampton.

What happened on August 13 Nat viewed as the sign appearing again, compelling him not to wait longer. That day, from early morning to late afternoon the Sun's appearance went from pale green to light blue with a hint of green to silvery white to polished silver with a prominent black spot, and in a gloomy light people stared at it and wondered. For more than an hour after sunset, the western horizon was defined by a curtain of brilliant scarlet. In Southampton and everywhere else the phenomenon was visible, again people were in awe, and again many worried that the Day of Judgement might be near.

On Sunday the 14th, with the Sun almost normal, anxious people flocked to the churches. At Barnes Meeting House, hundreds of whites and blacks came together from all directions, then separated. Outside at the grape arbor behind the church, Nat preached to the blacks. Inside the church, Sally's uncle George Washington Powell preached to the whites. And people went home. Later, some whites recalled that many of the blacks were wearing red sashes, scarves and other items.

On Sunday afternoon the 21st, the conspirators gathered at Cabin Pond to share a meal and make final plans. Present were not only Nat, Hark, Henry, Nelson and Sam, but also a resolute Will Francis (like Sam a slave of Nathaniel) and a reluctant Jack Reese. The insurgents basically planned to attack along a meandering route leading to Jerusalem, recruiting new men along the way, obtaining guns, gunpowder and ammunition, swords and knives, horses and mules. To Jerusalem other blacks could rally to the cause.

Leaving Cabin Pond near midnight in almost full moonlight, the men went to the Travis farm, where at about 2 a.m. the insurrection began with the killing of the Travis family. (As the men proceeded toward the nearby farm of Salathiel Francis, a slave boy began running through the woods to warn Nathaniel Francis, becoming the first of numerous slaves who would help spread the alarm and protect white people on this day.)

During the night and into the morning of the 22nd, slowly gathering strength, the slaves attacked whites at about 18 places (while bypassing the farms of some poor whites), the Rebecca Vaughan home along the Barrow Road being the last place where whites were killed. Along the insurrectionary path, the death scenes were shocking, particularly at Levi Waller's place, where the dead included at least 10 schoolchildren. All told, the insurgents had killed at least 57 white men, women and children, a majority of whom had attended services at Turner's Meeting House. Nat himself killed a young woman named Margaret Whitehead, beating her to death with a fence rail after his sword proved too dull for the task.

With approximately 60 mounted but weakly armed insurgents approaching Jerusalem, refugees were already streaming into town, while everywhere in Southampton the alarm was spreading and white people were fleeing to safe places or organizing armed patrols. (The postmaster had shakily scribbled a note and entrusted it to young Thomas Jones, who began an epic hard journey during which he rode three horses to death before he arrived in Petersburg, his message reaching Governor Floyd in Richmond during the night.)

At about noon, in what became known as the Battle of Parker's Field, the insurgents engaged in a brief but fierce fight with militiamen. Several blacks were killed or wounded, and the rest scattered. Nat and some of the men rode to the Cypress Bridge, which was already guarded, then roamed the countryside from one abandoned farm to another before heading to the Buckhorn slave quarters to pass a restless night. In summer heat and dust, the path of insurrection had covered about 30 miles.

At dawn on the 23rd, at the darkened home of Simon Blunt, the insurgents were met with a volley of gunfire killing or wounding several of Nat's men and dispersing the others while some of Blunt's slaves emerged from the kitchen house to fight for their master. A later bloody skirmish with militiamen at the Newitt Harris farm ended the rebellion. Nat, armed only with a dull sword, went into hiding, alone, near Cabin Pond.

The rebellion had indeed been crushed, but it took several days for people to realize it. Meanwhile, chaos prevailed throughout Southampton and its neighboring counties, down into North Carolina. Frightened whites fled to Jerusalem and Cross Keys and hastily fortified homes, abandoning farms to the care of slaves. More than a thousand refugees crowded into Jerusalem. Some 1,400 congregated at Cross Keys, surrounded by a guard of about 200 men.

By mid-week, hundreds of militiamen and armed civilians were entering Southampton. By week's end, Virginia militia General Richard Eppes commanded more than 3,000 men in Southampton, including about 300 federal soldiers from Fort Monroe and sailors and marines from two Navy warships anchored in Hampton Roads.

Amid great turmoil, in dozens of incidents, some militiamen and others began randomly killing mostly innocent slaves and free blacks. Many of the slayings were particularly brutal. It is not known how many blacks died during several days of white violence. The only published contemporary estimate was approximately 40-120, but the number might have been more. Brave white men – William Parker at the Jerusalem jail and Pitt Thomas at Cross Keys – defied angry mobs to protect black prisoners. Finally, on August 28, an outraged General Eppes sternly declared martial law, condemning the slayings and ordering an immediate end to the violence. Law and order were restored.

Many blacks were taken into custody, overcrowding the well guarded jail in Jerusalem. Some of the obviously innocent slaves were quickly released to their masters. Others were released following preliminary hearings before two magistrates. During the trials in the Court of Oyer and Terminer, court-appointed attorneys entered for all of the defendants pleas of "not guilty" to charges of "feloniously counseling, advising and conspiring with diverse other slaves to rebel and make insurrection, and taking the lives of diverse free white persons." All told, 15 slaves were acquitted, 12 were convicted and sentenced to be hung but were recommended for commutation and sale out of state, and 19 (including a woman) were convicted and sentenced to be hung. Before the sentences were carried out, Governor Floyd reviewed the transcripts of all of the trials. (Four free blacks were later tried in the Southampton Superior Court. One was convicted and hung, the others acquitted.)

For nine weeks, in Southampton and elsewhere, the relentless search for Nat continued, prolonging the fear and anxiety, deepening the impact of the failed rebellion.

After leaving Cabin Pond, Nat hid well. But on October 15, near his hiding place under a pile of old fence rails in the middle of a field, he was spotted by two slaves, who told the whites. The manhunt intensified. On the 27th, near his new "cave" inside a fodder stack in a field on Nathaniel's farm, he was spotted by Nathaniel, who fired his pistol, the bullet putting a hole in Nat's hat.

Finally, on the morning of October 30, emerging from concealment under the leafy branches of a fallen tree, Nat was captured at gunpoint by local farmer Benjamin Phipps, and surrendered his sword. Taken initially to the farm of Peter Edwards, where a local celebration began, Nat was then taken through the neighborhood, subjected to anger and scorn. The next day, he was taken to Jerusalem and jailed.

Silent in his cell after an initial interview by two magistrates, Nat agreed to talk to Thomas Gray, whom he knew. They met on November 1, 2 and 3, Nat telling his story while Gray listened, occasionally asking questions.

On the 5th, represented in the Court of Oyer and Terminer by attorney William Parker, Nat Turner, property of the estate of Putnam Moore, was tried by all of the county's magistrates. He pled not guilty, having declared to his counsel that he did not feel so. Convicted and sentenced to be hung on the 11th, Nat declined an opportunity to speak.

On the 11th, Nat was transported from the jail to the usual place of execution. There, he handed his Bible to a deputy sheriff, and then, amid a large but mostly quiet and somber crowd, he was hung.

In a letter written in November, Governor Floyd noted that according to the reports he had received from Southampton regarding the insurgents: "All died bravely."

AFTERMATH

The insurrection was brief and failed, but it shocked the nation, setting in motion forces which would fundamentally alter the course of American history, polarizing public opinion, diverting the American people away from the prospect of a widespread interracial war and leading to the Civil War.

On November 22, 1831, in Baltimore, Thomas Gray's pamphlet **The Confessions of Nat Turner** went on sale. More than 50,000 copies were soon in circulation, spreading the word about what had happened, assuring the fame of Nat Turner as a great villain or a great hero.

The dramatic 1831-32 session of the Virginia General Assembly produced the first – and last – free and full legislative consideration of gradual compensated emancipation ever conducted in the South. The debate was lively and very public. The legislators concluded that nothing could be done at that particular time, or should be attempted until the strong support of public opinion could be obtained, and not until some complex and costly plan could be contrived to accomplish the task. The legislators also acted to strengthen the state militia and discourage black preachers and religious meetings and blacks learning to read and write, with punishments also for whites helping the blacks.

In 1832, at Governor Floyd's request, College of William and Mary professor Thomas Dew reviewed the legislative debates, then authored a powerful report. With compelling statistics and reasoning, Dew argued against emancipation, contending that it would be ruinous to the economy and peace of Virginia, that slavery was in fact economically sensible and morally good, a benefit to all, including the slaves. Dew concluded that "the time for emancipation has not yet arrived, and perhaps it never will." Widely circulated, Dew's persuasive analysis became the prevailing opinion of the South.

In 1835, Alexis de Tocqueville (whose stagecoach traveled through Jerusalem in January of 1832), began publishing his classic **Democracy in America**. Regarding the "calamity" of slavery, he noted: "The danger of a conflict between the white and black inhabitants of the Southern states of the Union (a danger which, however remote it may be, is inevitable) perpetually haunts the imagination of the Americans like a painful dream."

Significantly, seven of Nat Turner's contemporaries in Southampton became notable in history:

Simon Blunt Jr. – A teenager when he helped repel the insurgents at the Blunt farm, he became a naval midshipman, served on the first ship of the United States Navy to circumnavigate the globe, and married a daughter of Francis Scott Key, author of the popular poem "The Star-Spangled Banner."

Fed Moore – He left Southampton as a boy. Sold several times and renamed, he experienced the worst horrors of slavery, eventually escaping to the North and going to England, where in 1856 abolitionists published his story – **John Brown: Slave Life in Georgia** – which fanned the flames of abolitionism in Britain and America.

Dred Blow – Sold by the Blow family, he became Dred Scott. In 1857, he was denied his freedom by the United States Supreme Court in a decision which shattered the Missouri Compromise and sharply increased tensions between the North and the South. After the decision, the Blow family bought their former slave and freed him, and a year later paid for his funeral.

James Rochelle Jr. – Son of Southampton's clerk of court in 1831, he became a naval midshipman, served under Commodore Matthew Perry during the Mexican War, then became one of the first graduates of the new United States Naval Academy in Annapolis. In 1856, he served on the USS Southampton during Perry's door-opening mission to Japan. As a Confederate naval officer, he witnessed the clash of the Monitor and the Merrimack, and served as the last commanding officer of the Confederate States Naval Academy. After the war, he helped to conduct surveys of the largely unexplored Amazon River, then returned home, a beloved local hero.

William Mahone – A boy in 1831, in manhood feisty little Billy Mahone graduated in 1847 from the new Virginia Military Institute, and became a civil engineer and eventually president of a railroad company. An ardent secessionist, he became a general in the Army of Northern Virginia. In 1864 at Petersburg, he became "The Hero of the Crater," his actions quickly closing the gap in the Confederate defense line. In 1865 at Appomattox, almost half of the men remaining in the battered Army of Northern Virginia were in brigades commanded by Mahone. After the war, he became the most powerful man in Virginia, a railroad tycoon, millionaire, political king-maker, Republican member of the United States Senate. When he died in 1895, his testament included this observation: "I never learned my wretched error, the awful blunder of the South, the curse of her institution of slavery and her traditions until I sat in the United States Senate, and day by day had borne in upon me the amazing significance of our form of government, what it meant, on what basis it was founded, how great and grand it was above any previous human effort, what it meant for humanity."

George Thomas – As a teenager, he and his family twice barely escaped the insurgents. He became a roommate of William Tecumseh Sherman at the United States Military Academy, and served gallantly in the Mexican War, formally honored by the grateful citizens of Southampton. During the

Civil War, the leading Union generals were Ulysses Grant, Sherman and Thomas – "The Rock of Chickamauga," whose actions at the Battle of Chickamauga in 1863 saved the Union army from disaster.

Anthony Gardner – One of the free blacks who left Southampton early in 1831, he became a Signer of the Liberian Declaration of Independence, served as a delegate to the Liberian Constitutional Convention and as three-term president of the Republic of Liberia.

Lightning Source UK Ltd.
Milton Keynes UK
UKOW02f0258170915

258777UK00003B/27/P